BALLET

From the First Plié to Mastery
An Eight-Year Course

BALLET

From the First Plié to Mastery
An Eight-Year Course

Anna Paskevska

Routledge
New York and London

Published in 2002 by
Routledge
29 West 35th Street
New York, NY 10001

Published in Great Britain by
Routledge
11 New Fetter Lane
London EC4P 4EE

Photography by Steven Hayes Rimlinger

Models: Emily Rose Cannon, Hanaan Bing-Canar, Meghan Angelos, Imani Mosley, Kathleen Telfer, Pablo Von Sternenfels, Julia Radominski, from the Academy of Movement and Music, Oak Park, IL. And Annika Sheaff, Ariane Baum, Jonathan Alsberry, from the Chicago Academy for the Arts, Chicago, IL.

10 9 8 7 6 5 4 3 2 1

Cataloging-in-Publication Data is available from the Library of Congress.

ISBN 0-415-94291-8

CONTENTS

ACKNOWLEDGMENT

Soon after arriving in the US in 1966, I looked for a dance studio to take class. Audrey Estes, at the Princeton Ballet Society, and a little later Mila Gibbons at the Appari Studio, asked me if I would like to teach. I had not envisioned teaching at that time but once in the studio felt like the proverbial fish in water, loving every moment. I knew the structure of the class and the sequencing of exercises. Improvising had always been easy for me so I could devise *enchaînements* on the spot. I followed the format and gamboled with my students to our mutual delight. Then followed years of discovery accompanied by a deepening respect and admiration for the process inherent in the classical technique of nurturing dancers.

In the last thirty-six years I have learned much and thank my students, past and present, for giving me the opportunity to hone my craft as a teacher.

Anna Paskevska
Chicago, 2002

Cleo Nordi 1899-1983

DEDICATION

Of all the teachers with whom I have studied, Cleo Nordi was the most enduringly influential in shaping my understanding of the classical technique. Under her tutelage I realized that the daily class is a continuum developing logically within its specific structure. Her classes were like a good meal: perfectly balanced in nutritional value, and filling without being overwhelming, leaving one with eager anticipation for the next. Nordi often said that ballet was like mathematics: two and two equals four—a correct position plus force equals a *pirouette*. Proper understanding of the function of the exercises leads directly to an appreciation of their role in shaping the muscles necessary for the execution of all the steps of the technique.

Because most young dancers are primarily concerned with the moment, with the immediate problem to be solved, with a step to be perfected, I had only a vague intimation of the import of her teaching. Only when I started teaching did I find my thoughts turning to the memory of her classes. Remembering her corrections, her explanations, and the pace of her classes, I began to gain an ever greater appreciation of the classical tradition and technique.

Nordi was born in Finland in 1899. Her mother was Russian, and her father was Finnish. She studied ballet with Nicolas Legat, first in St. Petersburg, and later, as a mature dancer, in London. She also studied Modern Dance in Germany and made her debut at the Paris Opera in 1925. In 1926, she joined Anna Pavlova's Company and toured with the group until its disbandment in 1931.

She taught in London for the Sadler's Wells Ballet School, the London Contemporary Dance Theatre, and the Essen Folkwang School under the direction of Kurt Jooss. Nordi's knowledge and experience of the classical technique had been enriched by exposure to modern dance concepts, just as mine was to be. She was able to explain the performance of a particular step not only from a classical viewpoint but also from a modern viewpoint, explaining physical implications of performing a step in a particular fashion.

During a visit to London in 1982, I spent an afternoon with Cleo Nordi at her apartment in Kensington. She served tea in her living room, and we talked about dance surrounded by memorabilia. Over the mantel, hung a portrait of Nordi by the Austrian painter Wolfgang Craig-Hainisch, who lent the picture to her during the last two years of her life. The fifty years since that portrait had been painted and a long illness had not marred the beauty of this eighty-year-old woman. When I stood up to say good-bye, she gave me a photograph of the painting and expressed pleasure and appreciation for the words I had written in the introduction to *Both Sides of the Mirror* in praise of her teaching. Little indeed for the years of patient nurturing she had given me.

Madame Nordi died the following year, in London, and I cherish the memory of our last meeting. Although she suffered from a terminal illness, she continued to teach in her Kensington studio until her death. Unknowingly, my students pay homage to her each time we perform the *révérence* that she too ended her classes with.

PREFACE

The education of the ballet teacher begins with her or his first *plié* as a student. Although teaching is not the goal at that time, many of us eventually make the transition from performer to teacher, and rely on the knowledge acquired during those early years.

Like passages of life, the transition from performer to teacher is a period of reevaluation. As a student, and later as a performer, I strove to improve my execution, and addressed my problems: how can I make my extension higher; what would make my balance more secure; how can I spin one more time? My concentration was directed inward, my concern was with my body and its specific limitations. When I became a teacher, my focus was directed outward. In the classroom I was faced with students whose body types were very different from my own. The conclusions I had reached to improve my technique were only somewhat useful. I had to acquire the skills to help my students with problems I had not encountered as a dancer.

Fortunately, training asserted itself without my conscious choice. Analysis followed later, and with it a true appreciation of my teachers and the classical tradition they had imparted. The tradition reached back to my teachers' teachers. Particularly influential were the principles that Nicolas Legat had passed on to Cleo Nordi. She often referred to him during our lessons, but more importantly she taught in the spirit he had instilled in his pupils. Another of his students, the English dancer Alan Carter, described Legat's teaching style: "He taught: to rethink, understand, and develop, but not to copy . . . . Technique is a living, growing thing, and must adapt and encompass new things . . . . A master must visualise perfection and transmit it to his pupils; this is classicism . . . . Legat's was the classical way."[1]

Nicolas Legat (1869-1937) graduated from the St. Petersburg Imperial Theatre School (now the Kirov) in 1888. Through his dancing career, which spanned twenty-five years, he was a faithful interpreter of many roles and a much sought-after partner of the acclaimed ballerinas of the day: "The talents of Nicolas were more suitable to those of the *demi-caractère* dancer, but his elegance and academic training enabled him to shine in romantic parts."[2]

He succeeded Christian Johansson (1817-1903), who had been his teacher, as ballet master of the Class of Excellence at the Imperial School and taught until 1914. At that time, he took a leave of absence from the Imperial Theatre to tour abroad with his wife. At the outbreak of World War I, they were performing in Paris and their return to Russia was a protracted and difficult journey.

Once there, Legat resigned from the Imperial Theatre and taught at the Bolshoi Theatre and School in Moscow. Subsequently he became associated with Akim Volinsky, a critic, and taught at the latter's Academy of Ballet. These were unsettled times in Russia, and Legat was never to regain his former prestigious position. In 1922, because of his wife's illness, they were granted a six-month leave abroad. About that time one of Legat's pupils, Agrippina Vaganova, was appointed in his place to a position that would shape the future of Soviet Ballet.

For a short time, Legat was ballet master for Diaghilev's Ballets Russes; then he settled in England and taught there until his death in 1937. Although his name was erased from the annals of Soviet dance history, his teaching influenced many of the dancers who later held prominent places in Soviet ballet as well as dancers who left Russia and continued their careers in Europe and America. Alexandra

---

1. John Gregory, *Nicolas Legat, Heritage of a Ballet Master* (New York: Dance Horizons, 1977), p. 19.

2. Ibid., p. 5.

Danilova wrote: "When I arrived in London with the Diaghilev Ballet I was thrilled because here was the teacher of my teacher, Madame Vaganova, and now I could study with this real master, Nicolas Legat."[3]

Legat's approach to teaching was grounded in the classicism of the nineteenth century, but he brought to it his own analytical talent and his deep understanding of the body. Because he understood the mechanics of movement, he was able to clarify many of the accepted ways of performing steps. Through the work of Vaganova, his theories became part of the mainstream of teaching in the Soviet Union.

In the years since Legat's death, the classical technique has evolved with unprecedented rapidity, but the precepts he advocated still hold true and are directly applicable to the process of nurturing a dancer today. Balanced alignment, subtle use of weight changes, and fluidity in execution are still qualities that distinguish a well-trained dancer. As Anna Kisselgoff remarked: "Ballet is about transitions as much as steps, not about stage pictures that can be removed like picture slides."[4]

Although I do not advocate a "system," the precepts followed throughout this book are based on the Russian School as developed by Nicolas Legat and taught by Cleo Nordi. These precepts are further tempered by my experience as a student at the Royal Ballet School in London and by direct application of teaching students of all ages for over thirty years.

These pages are written in the hope that, in the spirit of the master, they will encourage you to rethink, understand, and develop.

3. Ibid., p. ix.
4. Anna Kisselgoff, "Dance View," *The New York Times,* 8 March 1987, p. 12.

PART ONE
Use and Benefits of Classical Training

INTRODUCTION TO BALLET TECHNIQUE

This book is intended as a resource guide for teachers and would-be teachers of ballet, and modern dancers/teachers who want to gain a deeper understanding of the process of classical training.

While the relevancy of this work to ballet teachers is obvious, it may not be quite so clear in the case of modern teachers. All too often ballet is perceived primarily as a style, a perception that becomes a barrier to full appreciation of the technique. Before style, there is technique. Ballet is a system of physical education that fosters control, awareness, flexibility, and strength. It develops the musculature and maintains the physique in such an efficient and all-encompassing manner that all dancers can benefit from an involvement in the form. Indeed, a growing number of modern dancers take ballet classes and find them helpful in improving and maintaining their technique.

When stylistic differences are put aside, it is possible to look at all of today's dance disciplines in terms of their common contribution toward a specific goal: development of a supple musculature that will be responsive to choreographic demands. A thorough mastery of one idiom allows a dancer to adapt to a wide variety of different styles, as Nureyev and Baryshnikov have demonstrated by performing in works by José Limón, Paul Taylor, and Twyla Tharp.

Contemporary choreographers no longer work within the narrow confines of a single idiom, but use steps and configurations from all disciplines. Although it cannot be denied that the classical technique imposes a unique style, it is possible to transcend style and gain the physical benefits that ballet training offers.

The process through which ballet training achieves its goal is simple, albeit long in duration. The early years address control over the large, superficial muscle groups, like the quadriceps, but as training continues it calls into play the deeper muscle groups. The development of the inner musculature allows for an ever-increasing refinement in execution; the motions originate close to one's center and radiate outward through the limbs, rather than being initiated by the surface musculature. The classical technique provides the means to achieve subtle weight transference, centering, and managing the weight mass around the center of gravity when in motion. It also enhances the illusion one creates with movement—making the body appear light or heavy, or prolonging the time at the apex of a jump. Because these concerns are shared by all dancers, I hope that this book will prove useful to the modern dancer and teacher.

TERMINOLOGY

Before addressing the question of how the material in this book can be used, certain terms that are used throughout the text need to be defined. Terms not found here can be found in the glossary.

General

Craft and Technique. These two terms are often synonymous. They describe the totality of dance training. As students progress through the curriculum, they acquire proficiency in the *technique* or they learn the *craft*. Additionally, technique can refer to the correct execution of the steps and exercises of ballet, while craft presumes a broader knowledge, one that includes a familiarity with the history of dance as well as an appreciation of anatomy and kinesiology.

Style. The classical technique imposes a certain generic style because it requires a specific stance. The lengthening of the spine, the uplifted carriage of the head, and the turn-out of the legs all contribute to the "ballet look." In these pages, I use the word "style" to contrast with "technique." Style in this sense becomes a choreographic choice. We can talk about the Romantic style, characterized by a softness in the use of the arms and an emphasis on the ethereal. We can also contrast the Kirov and the Bolshoi styles. The former tends toward a lyrical interpretation, while the latter is broader and more athletic in its expression. Closer to home we have the Balanchine style, which distinguishes the dancers of the New York City Ballet from, for example, the dancers of the Joffrey Ballet. Thus, a style is not a method of training, but a particular interpretation of the classical technique, which usually emphasizes or exaggerates certain aspects of the technique.

Line. Like the term "conformation," which is used by breeders to describe dogs and horses, *line* attests to the training a dancer has received. The classical line requires a balance between body and limbs that conforms to the aesthetics of the technique. This subject will be discussed in greater detail in "Precepts of the Technique."

Principles. The underlying reasons that govern all classical movements. Generally, a principle is based on two considerations: aesthetic and physical. For example, head positions were devised with the audience as the focal point. Thus, the head turns this way and that in order to preserve the contact with the public—an aesthetic consideration. Additionally, the placement of the head helps to maintain equilibrium; therefore in many positions the head is tilted toward the supporting side—a physical consideration.

Vocabulary. All the steps of the technique. A glossary that defines all the vocabulary used in the book is provided.

Placement and Alignment. Although they may appear to describe the same thing, I use the word "placement" specifically to denote the balletic stance, whereas "alignment" refers to the configuration of bone upon bone in a more general way.

Form. Used not only to describe the shape of the movement, but also to define idiom. We are moving toward a homogenizing of dance techniques. It makes sense to discuss specific forms or idioms rather than compartmentalize ballet into sharp categories, such as classical, neoclassical, contemporary ballet, and so on.

Specialized

Arms. I have numbered the positions of the arms and *port de bras* in a manner that seems logical. The term *"allongé"* is used to describe lengthened positions in which the palm of the hand faces downward. The term is always followed by a further qualification, as in *allongé devant* or *allongé* in 3rd position, when both arms extend toward the front, the upstage arm originating in 5th position and the downstage one in 1st (which represents the 3rd position).

Arabesques. Three *arabesques* are referred to in this book. These positions are further qualified by the terms *croisée* (crossed) and *ouverte* (open). In first *arabesque*, the same arm as the supporting leg is extended forward. In second *arabesque*, the opposite arm to the supporting leg is extended forward. In third *arabesque*, both arms are extended forward.

Coupé and cou-de-pied. Often mistakenly interchanged, they actually mean very different things. *Coupé* describes a cutting motion. Its path of travel is downward, like the blade of a guillotine. The purpose of *coupé* is to free the nonworking leg for motion. The weight of the body transfers to the leg that executed the *coupé* and the other leg opens in whatever direction is necessary to execute the step that follows.

By contrast, *cou-de-pied* is merely a position. It indicates a place on the supporting leg where the working leg is held, heel resting on the ankle of the supporting leg.

Fondu and plié. Sometimes interchanged, these terms lose their specific character. I always use *fondu* in its primary definition: a composite movement that includes a *plié* and a *développé*. On the other hand, *plié* refers to a bending of the supporting knees or knee.

THE PROGRESSION OF BALLET TRAINING

This course of study covers eight years. Each chapter lists the vocabulary for the year, discusses the focus or emphasis for that particular year of study, and provides a sample lesson. The course can be roughly divided into three levels: elementary for years one—four, intermediate for years five and six, and advanced for years seven and eight.

The first four years are the most critical in establishing good habits and setting the foundation for all future progress. At the intermediate level the focus shifts slightly to the acquistion of vocabulary. During the final two years of study, execution of the vocabulary is perfected. Many students never reach the advanced stage because of their physical limitations, although they may be familiar with the entire vocabulary. This is not to say that they are not very fine dancers. After intermediate level has been mastered, subsequent individual progress is conditioned by ability and talent.

The progression of ballet training parallels the physical and intellectual development of growing children. Before age seven, children perceive and can cope with only gross motor movements. They have neither the physical ability to hold a position nor the concentration to follow through in a series of motions. Although creative movement and preballet classes for children are useful in teaching rhythm, a degree of control, and use of imagery, no attempt should be made to teach ballet technique or introduce movements that could be injurious to the joints.

Between ages seven and ten, the body gains in strength as the mind acquires the ability to concentrate for longer periods of time. While the seven-year-old will probably forget to stretch the knee while thinking about pointing the toes, the eight-year-old will be able to do both, and the nine-year-old will further be able to correct the position of the arms. Instilling correct habits is the principal goal of the early years of training. In time, turning the head or placing the arms in a specific position in relation to a leg movement becomes automatic. Accordingly, positions are taught

before transitions, single steps are mastered before they are linked in combination with other steps, the *en face* positions front, side, and back are clearly established before *croisé*, *effacé*, and *écarté* are introduced, and the first *port de bras* (from *bras bas* to 1st position, opening to 2nd, and returning to *bras bas*) is repeated to ensure correct basic use of the arms.

Through the years of training that are required to make a dancer, the acquisition of vocabulary is only one aspect of the total education. More importantly, the student builds musculature and develops a specific neuromuscular response, which make it possible to accelerate the acquisition of vocabulary after the initial four years of study.

APPLYING THE MATERIAL

Each sample class shows one instance in the use of the vocabulary slated for that year. During the first year or two, there will not be much variation in the individual lessons. Young children seem to respond well to routine and actually enjoy predictability. And, of course, the vocabulary is very limited, which precludes many "variations on the theme." Nevertheless, if the teacher demands attention to detail and praises correct execution, the students soon accept the teacher's priorities and take pleasure in striving for correct form.

As vocabulary for performance increases, more material may be covered in each class, although the structure of each lesson remains the same: barre, *port de bras*, center practice of barre exercises, adagio, *petit allegro*, *grand allegro*, and *petite batterie*. During the last two years of the elementary level, the emphasis is still primarily on the correctness of placement and alignment, and simple steps are used to illustrate the principles.

When the intermediate stage is reached in the fifth year the teacher can begin to base the barre exercises on the steps that will be introduced or practiced in the center. For example, if *ballonnés* will be practiced in the center, the barre can include *battement raccourci* in conjunction with *battement frappé*. This exercise introduces the action of directing the accent of the working leg inward, toward the supporting leg, that characterizes the execution of *ballonnés*.

Although the barre exercises and the combinations of center work can be more creative, the teacher must nevertheless conform to the rules of the classical technique when composing *enchaînements*. The rules of the technique either promote movement or make it easier. Therefore, in honoring the rules the teacher not only ensures that the sequences devised will be logical, but also that the student will learn the technique in its purest form. Thus, the rule that arms must pass through 1st before being raised to 5th or 4th position is applied to the execution of big jumps like *grand jeté en tournant* and *saut de basque en tournant*—the action of the arms actually facilitates the jump by helping to propel the body off the floor. Opening the arms to 2nd position at the conclusion provides a smooth ending for the movement.

Another rule concerns *pirouettes*. The general rule is that *pirouettes en dehors* finish with the working leg in back; *pirouettes en dedans*, in front. Like all rules this one has its exceptions: when *pirouettes en dehors* are executed in a series, the closing occurs in 5th position front because the end of one *pirouette* is also the beginning of the next *pirouette*, but the last *pirouette* of the series must close with the working leg in back. This rule arises from a physical consideration and takes into account the direction of the force exerted to produce the spin. By closing the leg in back after a *pirouette en dehors*, the direction of the force is not suddenly stopped but, without jarring, smoothly dissipated.

In the final two years of training, the teacher must guard against letting choreographic liberties creep into the combinations or detract from the classical line, mannerisms like "broken wrists"—hands that flip either up or down, breaking the long line of the arm—have little to do with the technique.

Erik Bruhn remarked during a conversation in London in 1982: "I do not teach style, I teach technique. Style belongs to choreography."[1] Unfortunately, students may often perceive their interpretation of a step as style, when it is merely a shortcut. Similarly, a teacher may indulge in idiosyncratic interpretation through habit or expediency. Many idiosyncratic interpretations and uses of the technique enhance classical movement and create interesting configurations, but this sort of creativity has no place in the classroom and cannot be applied to training methods.

Classical training promotes a widened range of motion through the use of strictly disciplined movements and positions. Because the progression of training is based on the physical development of the child, there can be no shortcuts during the initial years of study. Only when the child has reached the intermediate level can there be variations and adaptations to suit the particular aptitude of the student. After the age of eleven, a child may enter an accelerated program, whereas before that age, more harm than good will result from a too-rapid progression. Moving ahead too fast will ultimately compromise the goal of the craft, and may endanger the natural development of the child.

1. Private conversation between author, Erik Bruhn, and David Drew at the Royal Ballet School Cafeteria. Bruhn was teaching at that time (Spring 82) a class of senior boys.

FUNDAMENTALS FOR THE BALLET TEACHER

STUDENT CONDUCT

Learning ballet is wonderful for children even if they never become dancers. It is wonderful because it teaches discipline, grace, and manners. I had occasion recently to observe some classes given by Martha Mahr at her school in Miami. Miss Mahr began each lesson with a procession of the children, who walked in line as they entered the studio and formed a semi-circle to curtsy before proceeding to their place at the barre. Children who arrived late first made their apologies to Miss Mahr before joining the others at the barre.

When I remarked on the politeness of her students, she laughed and said: "They may not become dancers, but they will learn good manners!" The charming formality of the children's entrance into the studio reminded me of my days as a student, when we always curtsied to the teacher when entering or leaving the classroom. Although my young students line up to say goodbye to me after each lesson, I had not enforced a formal beginning to the class. After seeing Martha Mahr's class, I adopted her custom. Now my students march into class, holding the head high and pointing the toes with each step.

Formalizing the behavior of children within the walls of the studio has several advantages besides simply teaching manners. It sets the studio apart from other environs; it is not a big space like the gym, where they can run, jump, and scream. It is a place in which to concentrate in silence, to listen attentively, and to learn something very special. A formal entrance into the studio establishes the tone required for concentration.

After all, a truly disciplined classroom is one in which the teacher does not have to remind the children to be quiet. Discipline is not an end in itself; it simply helps foster an atmosphere conducive to work.

Uniformity of clothing also contributes to formality in the studio and helps to distinguish one group from another. Girls wear a leotard (a different color can be used for each level), pink tights—except for the first two elementary levels, for which white ankle socks are worn—and pink ballet slippers. The boys in the lower levels can wear short shorts and T-shirts, and later, black tights, white T-shirts (tucked into the ballet belt), white socks, and white shoes. The hair must be securely pinned away from the face and the neck. The complete attire is designed to reduce fussing during class, so that the students can concentrate on what they are doing.

TEACHER CONDUCT

Whatever the students' age, the ballet class imposes a natural progression, a rhythm, that provides a predictable structure. This predictability has both advantages and disadvantages. Although young students may find barre work boring, they know that eventually it will be time to do something they enjoy, like *pirouettes* or jumps.

The rote aspect of ballet training can be minimized by providing a task within the exercise that will absorb the student and demand concentration. The task can be very simple—pointing the toes, stretching the knees, holding the arm in a specific position. The teacher initially places the limb in the correct position, reminds the students when attention begins to slacken, and praises them when they show real effort. This process builds pride among the students and provides a short-term goal that is praiseworthy.

From the beginning of training, the correct French terms are used and their meaning explained. That way the teacher can ask the students to demonstrate a step or exercise as well as explain what it means. Through this process, students learn not only the execution of a step, but also its dynamics. For example, when performing *battement frappé*, the flexing and stretching action is coupled with a strong outward thrust. Children understand the action of hitting; when they are told that *frapper* means "to hit," they can relate the ballet movement to a familiar action and remember the exercise as well as execute it with the proper intent.

It is important for the teacher to remember that, at the elementary level, the execution of the vocabulary will obviously be less than perfect. As training continues the corrections will gain in subtlety: second-year students are doing well when they are able to land in an *assemblé* with both feet touching the floor simultaneously; third-year students will be expected to point the feet in the air; fourth-year students should begin and end in a clean 5th position.

Through the intermediate and advanced levels an increasingly analytical approach can be adopted, but analysis must never be purely theoretical. Ballet is a kinetic art and all corrections should be followed by an appropriate illustration. For example, if a student is having trouble keeping the thigh turned out during a *fondu* exercise, the problem can be explored again during the next exercise, *battement frappé,* by directing particular attention to the position of the leg on the *cou-de-pied* and monitoring the outward thrust.

All exercises serve to illustrate the basic concepts of the technique (this will be discussed in greater detail in "Precepts of the Technique" and can be used at anytime by the teacher to emphasize whatever aspect of execution seems to require attention. If approached in this manner, class becomes individualized, even if there are thirty people in the studio. Each student, besides working as a member of the group and therefore dealing with general directives from the teacher, will also be concentrating on individual problems. If the individual correction was carefully explained initially, subsequent reminders can take the form of catchwords, such as "Suzie, elbow" or "John, thigh," and Suzie will know that she has dropped her elbow, John that he has lost his turn-out.

It is not clear if dancers start out with a greater capacity for self-criticism than other people or if they develop it through the training. Although a critical eye is essential, too much self-criticism can eventually inhibit the dance quality of movements. To keep training from sinking into a morass of technicalities and to encourage a little freedom of movement, at least one combination during class should allow students free expression of movement. At the elementary levels, simply running and leaping across the room is sufficient. In the intermediate levels, the combination may be more technical and include *pirouettes.* By the advanced levels, challenge becomes the core of enjoyment and combinations should include an element to be conquered.

The tone of the lesson is set by the teacher. A serious approach does not preclude enjoyment and humor. Often humor can give welcome relief from intense concentration, allowing for a renewal of energy. The priorities set by the teacher are going to be accepted by the students. If the teacher is interested only in how many *pirouettes* the students can execute without regard for the form, in all likelihood they will twirl away in varying approximations of the real shape. Similarly, if the teacher allows talking in class, the students will chatter between exercises, jeopardizing their own and others' concentration. Like the formal entry into the studio and the applause or individual curtsy at the end of the lesson, formalized conduct during class provides an atmosphere conducive to working and learning.

PARENT INVOLVEMENT

Parents are a necessary, if mixed, blessing. They can be supportive and indispensable or, if allowed, create dissent and bad feeling among the students. It helps to set out guidelines for parents. You are the expert in this field, and that needs to be established. If you decide to put little Margie in Level One, then that is where little Margie should go, even if her mother insists that Margie belongs in Level Three because, at the ripe age of seven, she has been dancing for five years. (Placing children in the correct level can be a very tricky business if they come from another school. A placement class is useful and can avoid embarrassment later.)

Parents often ask to observe classes. With new students in the lower levels the rules need to be a little stricter than with older students, who will not be distracted by visitors. In the latter case, observation by parents, family, and even friends is at the discretion of the teacher. For the former, one or two open-class days can be scheduled for each semester. At the beginning of each year the closed doors allow the teacher to establish a relationship with the students as well as set certain rules for conduct.

Then, there is the ubiquitous school recital. If the intention of the school is to train dancers, spending a half year of class time to rehearse routines is worse than a waste of time; it cheats the students of hours of valuable learning experience. If the recital is an economic necessity, time to rehearse should be set aside that does not impinge on class time.

At recital or demonstration time, parents come into their own. Their talents can be enrolled in a variety of ways, from sewing costumes to keeping order backstage. If a non-competitive atmosphere is maintained, the experience can be very happy for everyone.

TEACHING YOUNG BOYS

The vocabulary for boys and girls is the same through the elementary levels. Special classes for boys are not necessary until a high intermediate level has been reached. A men's class typically includes greater emphasis on building strength. This can be achieved through the use of *demi-plié* and *relevé* in conjunction with *développés*. One such exercise is *développé*, the supporting leg in *demi-plié* as the working leg unfolds; *relevé* to *demi-pointe*, working leg *passé* to open into the next *développé*. This sequence is executed to the front, side, and back and is followed by a *passé* to *développé devant* and *grand rond de jambe en dehors*. Then the entire sequence is repeated beginning in back, with *grand rond de jambe en dedans* at the end.

It is necessary for male dancers to build strength for two reasons: they are expected to be able to lift their partner, and the male vocabulary consists of jumps and beats that require great elevation. Therefore, a men's class will be "heavier" than a woman's, in other words, it will include longer combinations with more emphasis on *demi-plié* and a greater number of *grands battements* and *fondus* at the barre. Center work will stress *pirouettes* of all kinds, including *grandes pirouettes*. Jumped conbinations will include beats and *tours en l'air*.

Although it is necessary to build strength in the upper body as well as the legs, it is not a good idea to encourage boys to enter into weight lifting programs as an adjunct to ballet training. The type of musculature developed through weight lifting generally contradicts the type desirable for a dancer. Overly powerful surface muscles tend to bind the joints, preventing a full range of motion. Furthermore, weight lifting usually develops short muscles, the kind that, although strong, lack elasticity. Thus, not only does the full range of motion become inhibited, but also the look of the dancer ceases to be aesthetically pleasing. Push-ups are an exception and can be included in lessons, either before class begins or after barre work is completed.

However, once a young boy becomes serious about ballet training, he should consider cutting back on other sports activities. Running foreshortens the hamstrings, wrestling develops the kind of strength that is inapplicable to dance, horsemanship uses thigh muscles in a way that precludes good turn-out—as does ice-skating—and gymnastics encourages curvature of the spine and overdevelopment of the pectoral muscles. While ballet may benefit the performance of all these sports, the converse is not true because ballet requires a very specific use of the musculature. The one exception to these many taboos is swimming—in moderation.

It is also not advisable to allow boys to do parterning that involves lifting before they are fifteen or sixteen years old and have developed a certain degree of strength. Of course, some fourteen-year-olds may be physically ready to perform simple lifts, but caution and discretion should be exercised.

These considerations presuppose that boys start dancing at about the same age as girls. Unfortunately, most often boys do not start ballet classes until their teens—sometimes late teens—after they have participated in a variety of athletic programs at school. Unlike younger children, late beginners do not have time to develop the needed neuromuscular responses in a systematic way. Teachers must also address the natural impatience of older students, who want to move faster through the curriculum than their kinetic understanding allows. Nevertheless, achieving the classically correct line is more important than learning many steps. Basic classes that present the material in a clear, straightforward way are best suited to informing older beginners. Repeating a simple sequence many times will give them the opportunity to work on improving execution, rather than worrying about what comes next. Once this correctness is achieved, the lessons can move at a brisker pace.

POINTE WORK

Studies in the fields of sports medicine and child development give ample evidence of the dangers of premature *pointe* work. Before young girls are put on *pointe* the foot must be strong enough to support the weight of the body, which requires a strong arch and ankle. Strength in the hip joint and the spine is also needed in order to stand on one's toes. This strength allows the stress to be distributed through the major joints and provides the support essential for safety.

Prior to age twelve, caution and good judgment should guide the teacher in introducing *pointe* work. As a rule, four years of ballet training are required as preparation for the musculature to assume the correct stance on *pointe.* Initially, only movements on both feet should be executed on *pointe,* such as *échappé, sous-sus, assemblé,* and *bourrée.*

Both parents and children must be educated in the selection of the *pointe* shoe. The vamp must be long enough to cover the joints of the toes, and the shoe snug enough to prevent slippage. Protection of the joints is especially needed for children with very high insteps; they must wear shoes that have at least a four-inch vamp. Ironically, it is the children with the most beautiful arches who have the most problems at the beginning. Their feet tend to be weaker than the stubbier, less-flexible ones, and they will probably need to spend a longer period of time practicing the steps with the support of the barre.

As with the general training, a slow, careful approach to *pointe* work ultimately yields the best results. It gives the muscles time to develop and ensures safety by allowing a close monitoring of alignment throughout the acquisition of the vocabulary.

MUSIC

A pianist can make or break a ballet class. Unfortunately, there is no way of forestalling disasters because competency as a musician does not ensure competency as an accompanist. However, there are some guidelines: pianists must have a certain sympathy for the dance, they must have a memorized repertoire to avoid leafing through scores, and they must be willing to learn. It also helps greatly if they are able to improvise.

After these initial factors are established, the pianist must become familiar with the ballet vocabulary. The music must fit the movement in terms of dynamics and should reflect the quality or mood of the exercise or *enchaînement.* It is certainly worthwhile to invest time and patience in a pianist who is really interested in becoming an accompanist.

If a pianist is not available, there are numerous CDs for ballet class on the market. Jay Distributors has a good selection and Princeton Book Company, Publishers, carries a CD my pianist, Olga Meyer, and I put together. Olga has been playing for ballet classes for twenty years and is sensitive to the needs of dancers, the tempi are steady, there is a clear introduction and conclusion to each band, and she has included some wonderful adaptation from the operatic repertoire.

It is a good idea to be totally familiar with the CDs to be used in class, so that specific sections are easily found, and to always have several selections on hand for needed variety.

Teaching ballet is a very personal affair. There is no substitute for genuine concern grounded in a thorough knowledge of the craft. Without knowing students outside the classroom, we can still sense who they are and how they relate to people, predict how they will react to criticism or praise, and apprehend the degree of commitment we can expect. Just as the student is naked in front of the teacher, so is the teacher stripped of pretensions in front of the students. Ballet is a revealing art: movement, unlike words, cannot lie.

---

*See the Discography for a select list of ballet records with album numbers.

5th position, arms in 1st position

The wisdom of classical ballet training resides in its inclusiveness. It develops a long, lean musculature and extends the range of motion accessible to most people. The technique is also beautifully logical, basing its precepts on the natural laws governing the human potential for motion.

It has often been stated by detractors of classical ballet that the art form is unnatural and that it deforms and distorts the body. I would like to offer an opposite view. We have many drugs that cure disease yet when taken unwisely can kill the user. Similarly, although less dramatically, ballet training *can* cause physical problems if the movements of its vocabulary are taught incorrectly, but if the full import of the training method is understood, the technique widens range of motion, refines and stylizes physical actions, and produces the characteristically harmonious lines of the art.

Any technique that uses the body as its instrument must be based on inescapable physical factors if it is to promote the well-being of its practitioners; ballet training is no exception. The rate of growth, muscular functions, and an unbalanced approach to ballet training are issues that cannot be ignored in an age when pyrotechnics are encouraged and valued in a performer. The technique develops a balanced musculature only when exaggerations are not indulged or encouraged in the growing/learning child. To retain this musculature demands of the mature artist continuing awareness of alignment. The most common exaggerations are forced turn-out, overcrossed fifth position, and hyperextension in the hip joint area and the diaphragm.

The ballet class serves to foster and maintain both strength and flexibility in the dancer. When one aspect overshadows the other the result is a dancer who can raise a leg to 160 degrees, but cannot jump two inches off the floor, or who has so hyperextended the ligaments protecting the joints that there is constant danger of injury. Conversely, a dancer who has built tremendous strength may have done so to the detriment of mobility. When the conventions that prescribe the motions and lines of the art form are honored, stylistic as well as physical exaggerations can be avoided and the clarity of classical line preserved. At best, exaggerations result in mannerisms that deny access to the full range of expressiveness inherent in the technique; at worst, these exaggerations cause misalignment, predisposition to injury, and, even if injury is avoided, a shortened performing life.

BODY AND ALIGNMENT

The stylistic conventions of the classical vocabulary are directly related to physical considerations. The requirement of turning out makes it necessary to rearrange the body's weight around the center—positions of the head, shoulders, and arms (which can also be viewed as stylistic) are governed by the need to maintain equilibrium and minimize the effort inherent in all motions. The precepts of the technique are far from being mere posturing. A movement executed correctly, from the stylistic standpoint, is actually easier to perform because the physical configuration is designed to center the body's energy.

Nevertheless, some physiques are better suited to perform the classical vocabulary than others—it is easier for these body types to create the lines the technique demands. The apparent unsuitability of less-than-perfect physiques should not be a deterrent to ballet training, which is powerful enough to reshape the body if the process is started at an early age. Furthermore, the spirit and the will to dance more than compensate for physical disadvantages, many a great dancer has begun life in the art as an ugly duckling.

Body Type

We can classify body type into three broad categories, each requiring a slightly different treatment. The first has short ligaments, that allow little mobility in the joints, and short muscles that prevent the legs from stretching out and the feet from pointing fully. A person with this body type should be encouraged to perform stretching exercises every day. The execution of all movements must be monitored to forestall any further shortening of the musculature. Strain, which often results from overexertion, must be directed away from the areas where it is likely to cause further problems. This subject is discussed in more detail in the sections on Tension and Stress and Isolation.

The second is the opposite of the first: the ligaments and muscles are long, which allows too much movement in the joints and creates muscular weakness. Although this type may seem to be better suited to ballet the challenges facing it are no less arduous. Motions need to be contained, further hyperextension

avoided, and alignment closely supervised until a strong musculature has been built.

The third is the most balanced. Although the joints allow a wide range of motion, they are fully supported by ligaments that are neither too short nor too long, so that hyperextension is less likely to occur. Nevertheless, the temptation to push children endowed with this physique faster than the others must be resisted. The same considerations applicable to the other two body groups are relevant here. Alignment must be the first concern, strain must be avoided, and strong connections in the joints and spine must be developed before positions and steps that tax the physique are introduced.

All body types strive toward the same goal, classically true line, albeit from different angles. In order to achieve an untrammeled classical line, attention must be given to the verticality of the body, produced by alignment of the spine, upright positioning of the pelvis, alignment of the legs (hip joint, knee, ankle) and their relation to the pelvic area, and the relation of arms to shoulders and torso. Neither turn-out nor high extensions must be forced until the inner musculature has gained the strength to support the motions. Arm positions and transitions, with the accompanying head positions, must be learned concurrently with the *pas* of the technique. If these considerations are addressed during the first years of study, students will develop the long and supple musculature that enables them to execute the classical vocabulary with fluidity and grace.

Classical Line (*Arabesque*)

Line

Classical line, as the term implies, is characterized by its length, purity, and simplicity. The feet are pointed to create the illusion of a longer leg, the neck is lengthened in order to maintain a regal carriage, the arms are held to emphasize their maximum span, yet they are kept slightly rounded to retain their softness. Classical line creates harmonious configurations that are pleasing to the eye. Anything that detracts from the purity of line can be termed unclassical. Classical line is achieved not only by the correct placement of body and limbs, but more significantly through an inner tension guided by an aesthetic sense, which extends the line beyond the dancer's physical limits. By virtue of the aesthetic values that govern the execution of classical vocabulary, ballet shares in the broader cultural traditions of the Western World.

Classical line is much more than a mere stylistic attribute. After all, style changes, and there are numerous styles at any given period in history that affect the execution of the technique for a time. But the purity of the line has prevailed; it is the factor that distinguishes ballet from other dance forms and the superior performer from the merely adequate. It can be perceived as the heart of the technique.

Tension and Stress

Athletic activity requires tension. In classical ballet tension not only enhances movement but is used to link steps into coherent phrases. We need only look at a dancer like Baryshnikov to appreciate the meaning of tension. When he runs prior to a leap, for example, every muscle in his body is activated in anticipation of the leap. It is directed and controlled tension, yet as natural as the tension of a cat when it readies itself for a pounce. This kind of tension can also be described as energy and differs in quality from that found in other types of athletic activities. Dance energy is dynamic, directed outward from the center through the limbs. An integral part of dance action is to disguise the effort inherent in the action, to reorganize and translate it into pure energy.

On another level, the tensing and releasing of muscles create the musculature needed to execute the vocabulary. Both tensing and releasing have to occur in order to perform fluid motions—without tension there is no motion, yet constant tension without release creates stress. Therefore, both the effort and its rechanneling should be addressed at one and the same time.

Stress comes from misdirected effort, which in turn, is generally the result of basic misalignment—the body habituates to compulsive responses. Misalignment must be corrected at its source, along the spinal column. Most beginners, sometimes even more advanced students, tend to perceive movement as originating in the limbs. They strain because they bypass the help available from the back, pectoral, and pelvic area muscles.

If a dancer holds the hand in a strained, ungainly fashion, the correction "relax your fingers" is useless without the additional rectification of the position-tension between the shoulder blades and the realignment of the shoulder, so that the stress is absorbed and redistributed. If 5th position, the solid base from which movement can originate, is overcrossed, an aligned stance is impossible. Stress will occur in other parts of the body to compensate for the displacement.

For many important reasons it is pertinent to make posture the first consideration in training. Which brings us to the main culprit that creates misalignment.

Tucking-Under

Tucking-under is probably the most common mistake among dancers. In an effort to achieve a straight back, in the vain hope of disguising a larger than desired posterior, in the strain of lifting a leg, the response more often than not is to tuck under.

Unfortunately, this posture has extremely far-reaching negative results: it shifts the pelvis from a centered, balanced placement atop the femoral head; it inhibits the muscles around the hip joint, which precludes free outward rotation in that joint; it affects the rest of the spinal verticality, setting up areas of resistance that must be overcome before movement is possible; and it displaces the

Wrong

Right

weight of the body, causing the knees to absorb a great deal of strain.

When the body is correctly aligned, weight is carried through the center of the joints; when misalignment occurs the weight presses against the outward ligaments. The joints become vulnerable as they are no longer protected. Another long-term result of misalignment is the building of muscles that detract from classical line. Whether we work correctly or incorrectly, we still make muscles in the process. It is far easier, although sometimes it requires more patience, to learn the vocabulary correctly at the outset than to reeducate the musculature once bad habits have become ingrained.

The classically straight back is achieved by minimizing the natural curvatures of the thoracic and lower dorsal areas. This repositioning is supported by the deep muscles of the spine as well as the abdominals, and is made possible by the centeredness of the pelvis. Like turn-out, the straight back position takes years to develop fully, and again like turn-out, the process should not be forced lest it create areas

of stress that will require correction later. Of course sway-backs should be corrected at the very beginning of training, but the sway-back cannot be corrected by tucking under. Rather, a lengthening downward of the sacro-iliac, a balanced position of the pelvis over the hip joint (head of the femur), and a forward stance should be encouraged, and maintained in the first years of training, gaining verticality as the body gains strength.

VOCABULARY AND PLACEMENT

Within the vocabulary of training can be found all the needed components for the execution of choreography. Each time a new way of performing a movement is contemplated a question should be asked: Does this serve the aim of the technique or is it a choreographic indulgence?

Choreographers have poetic license to use both the dancer and the technique in any way they choose. Teachers on the other hand are duty-bound by the rules of technique to give their students a solid knowledge of the craft

13

and to lead them toward becoming expressive interpreters. This duty requires recognition of the physical implications of a movement. Therefore, forcing turn-out or a "perfect" 5th position, or encouraging high extension, should be eschewed until the child has developed the strength to cope with the positionings without distortion.

Turn-Out

"Winged foot" or *sur le cou-de-pied*

Pointe tendue

Beginning with only a 45-degree opening, strength in the hip joint will be fostered. Turning out will gradually increase until, by the fourth year, a full opening to 90 degrees is possible. When the turn-out is firmly held in the hip joint, a further outward movement in the ankle joint can be expected. Mobility in the ankle allows the foot to be "winged," a position introduced with *frappé* and *petit battement sur le cou-de-pied* exercises. When the student can achieve winging without pronation, a perfect 5th position has been attained.

Turn-out *always* begins in the hip joint, with the rest of the leg in alignment. Special care and attention is directed to the knee joint each time turn-out is increased; the ligaments must be protected while the musculature is being developed.

Elementary position *sur le cou-de-pied*

Extension

In the classical technique all exercises address both strength and flexibility, contracting some muscles while stretching others. Some exercises are designed to emphasize one aspect over the other, but one specific exercise, *battement fondu*, can be used for either, depending on the intent of the teacher and the focus of the lesson. Performed no higher than 45 degrees, it builds strength; when the leg is lifted to 90 degrees and higher, it promotes extension.

An emphasis on high extensions too early in the training detracts from correct placement and the strength-building qualities of some exercises. Both are needed not only to achieve extension but for the execution of allegro: to get off the floor requires strength; to land requires placement, not only for safety's sake but also to maximize the ability to link steps into coherent phrases.

It is important in the beginning to nurture control and strength in the hip joint and spine by limiting extensions to 90 degrees.

Nevertheless, stretching exercises should be included in the class, either before barre work (on warm days) or after barre has been completed. In a physically active society, children are involved in athletics from an early age. As a result they often develop shortened muscle groups that prevent full straightening of the knees. Very stiff children should be encouraged to do stretching exercises at home.

Isolation

"Isolation" is a term used primarily by jazz dancers, but a discussion of this concept is not out of place in a book about ballet technique. When we move the leg without a sympathetic motion of the pelvis, lift an arm without also raising the shoulder, lift or turn the head without displacing the torso, we are in fact isolating the prime mover from the supporting structure. The ability to isolate is essential in order to provide freedom of movement. If we look at the exercises of the technique we see that they all involve isolation. Any motion is accompanied by an immobilisation of one part of the body or another to provide stability for the action, much like walking, where one leg provides the support while the other steps forward.

In the early years of training, a strict verticality of the body nurtures the ability to isolate at the same time that it allows the inner musculature to gain in strength in order to sustain the isolation. As the purpose of training is to provide the body with freedom of mobility, the concept of isolation is important because it promotes harmony of motion and an interrelatedness of muscular response without compulsive dependence.

Port De Bras

The correct use of the arms is probably one of the most difficult aspects of ballet training to impart to young students. The positions and transitions must be taught from the beginning to forestall the assumption that the use of arms is secondary to the vocabulary of the legs.

It is neither accidental nor capricious that during barre work arms are generally held in second position. If correct shape is preserved

Port de bras. The humerus is rotated inward in the shoulder socket. The rotation causes the elbow to be uplifted, then the lower arm is rotated outward in order to continue the line created by the upper arm. The hand faces front.

ARM POSITIONS

Bras Bas

1st position with the head slightly inclined

Bras bas épaulé

2nd position *en face*

3rd position

4th position *en l'air*

4th position *devant*

5th position

3rd position *allongé*

2nd position *allongé*

18

EPAULEMENT

Croisé and *effacé* qualify positions to the front and back. *Epaulé* further qualifies *croisé* positions and indicates the use of the arms and shoulders in a complementary fashion. *Ecarté* only qualifies positions to the side.

Croisé devant

Croisé derrière

Croisé devant épaulé

Croisé derrière épaulé

Effacé devant

Effacé derrière

Ecarté devant

Ecarté derrière

20

First *arabesque*

First *arabesque croisée*

Second *arabesque*

Second *arabesque croisée*

Arabesque ouverte with arms in 3rd *allongé*

Arabesque ouverte with arms in 2nd *allongé*

Arabesque croisée with arms in 3rd *allongé*

the position activates muscles of the torso, helps maintain verticality and balance, and introduces the elegance of carriage that characterizes classical ballet. When arms are correctly used they not only enhance motion, but also provide powerful support for jumps and turns.

Arms are as energized as legs, and although the muscles are tensed during action, the arms must not show stress or strain. To achieve fluidity and ease of execution the impulse and support for all actions of the arms comes from the torso, not the deltoids. Reliance on the back and chest muscles allows for stress-free transitions and harmony of motion.

Epaulement

The positions of the arms and shoulders, which define and qualify positions of the legs, are called *épaulement* (*épaules* is the French word for shoulders). These positions are governed by the twin rules of opposition and complement. The pose is oppositional when the shoulder and arm opposite to the front leg are emphasized (e.g. right leg, left arm); the pose is complementary when the same shoulder and arm as the front leg are emphasized.

The dancer's relation to the audience begins, *en face*, fully facing, and alters to *croisé* or *effacé, which qualify motions and positions to the front and back, or écarté,* which qualifies motions and positions to the side. Another term, *épaulé*, is generally used in conjunction with the position *croisé*, an oppositional pose. If the same arm as front leg is emphasized, however, the position becomes complementary and is called *croisé-épaulé*.

The concepts of opposition and complement are at the very foundation of classical style. They help to organize the body's weight, facilitate weight transference, and allow for the use of stylistic subtleties in adagio and allegro work.

Pirouettes

Some dancers turn more easily than others, but there is no reason why everyone in due time cannot perform effective, beautiful *pirouettes*. One rule is basic: *pirouettes en dehors*

(outside turns) close with the working leg in back; *pirouettes en dedans* (inside turns) close with the working leg in front. Like all rules, this one has exceptions, but when students first learn *pirouettes* the rule must be firmly instilled before the exceptions are introduced.

Beyond the mystique of turning there are two definite components to a spin: balance and impetus, or force. The dancer assumes a stable position, then applies force to create the spin. The same principles govern the execution of all *pirouettes*—those in the usual *retiré* position and the *grandes pirouettes* in the big poses. The only difference between them is the manner of preparation.

Preparation for *pirouettes en dehors* from 5th position.

Preparation. From 5th position (*en dehors* the working leg is in front; the reverse for *en dedans*), the weight is evenly distributed on both legs; the push off is also from both legs, the working leg pressing into the floor before quickly lifting into a *retiré* position.

From 4th position, the weight is on the front (supporting) leg, although the back leg maintains pressure on the floor. The pressure into the floor builds the necessary torque to create the spin, or *pirouette*. For *pirouettes en*

Impetus: Creating a torque for *grande pirouette* from 2nd position

Preparation for *grande pirouette en dedans* from 4th position

dehors the width of the fourth position, heel on the floor, is the same as when the leg is extended to a *pointe-tendue*. For *pirouettes en dedans* the 4th position is a little wider; for *grandes pirouettes* it is further increased.

The preparation prepares the dancer to perform the following movement, and is not simply a position one assumes arbitrarily. It must place the body in the most favorable position to begin the spin with as little adjustment as possible. Therefore, the body must be aligned over the supporting leg and the hips and shoulders squared off to each other. In 5th position the body is already placed centrally, but in 4th position the body's weight must be kept over the front leg.

The width of the 4th position is further increased for *grandes pirouettes*. In contrast to the preparation for regular *pirouettes*, the wider position will place the center of the body behind the supporting leg. This positioning is necessary because the wide 4th provides the extra impetus needed for *pirouettes* in big poses. Even more importantly, the wide 4th allows for the body's necessary shift forward when assuming the *arabesque* or *attitude*. The distance created by the wide fourth between the position in the preparation and the pose of the *pirouette* allows a smooth transition into the pose without the danger that the strong push off the floor and the height of the leg propel the body beyond the supporting leg. (For a more detailed discussion on *pirouettes* see Paskevska *Both Sides of the Mirror*.)

Impetus. There are two sources of impetus needed to produce a spin: the pressure of the feet onto the floor, which creates a torque, and the arms, which direct force into the shoulders. The use of this force is based on a strict rhythm, a fast "and-one." On "and" the working arm opens to 2nd position; on "one" the *relevé* on the supporting leg occurs and the position of the spin is assumed. In *pirouettes en dehors* the arms open directly to 2nd position. In *pirouettes en dedans* the front arm opens to 2nd, then both arms rise to 5th position. In other words, at the instant the outward force produced by the arm is redirected into the body, the dancer enters into the spin by doing a *relevé* on the supporting leg while the working leg assumes the desired position.

Position during *pirouette en dehors* or *en dedans*

Balance. A centered preparation places the body in a favorable position to assume the spin and to maximize the action of the torque. At the moment the working foot leaves the floor equilibrium becomes the main concern. One can even say that equilibrium is the main concern throughout, that all the actions preceding the spin are so directed. Thus, the centeredness of the preparation, the alignment of shoulders and pelvis, and a steady contact with the floor through the supporting leg are maintained. It must be noted that gravity exerts a backward pull on the body, which is overcome by keeping the weight forward over the supporting hip and using the head to spot.

Efficiency. The position in which the turn occurs must be assumed as quickly and as economically as possible; all motions not directly related to producing the spin should be avoided. This final concern is especially relevant for the execution of *grandes pirouettes*, when both the arms and the working leg must assume the position for the spin without a "wind-up" at the outset of the turn.

Like any movement in the classical technique, the aim of a *pirouette* is not to go around a central axis as many times as one can, but rather to create an aesthetically pleasing image which happens to revolve.

Arabesques

Placement in arabesques always has been rather controversial, separating teachers into two camps: the "square-hips" adherents and the "open-hips" proponents. In a historical context, keeping the hips perfectly "square" became impossible once leg extensions began to rise above 90 degrees. Teachers of the Russian school realized this fact as early as the 1920s and encouraged an open-hip position. The English school, whose curriculum was set by Enrico Cecchetti, adopted the square-hip position and has adhered to it until very recently. There are signs that the allegiance of English dancers is shifting with the influx of Soviet teachers who now are members of the faculty. In America, the question has never really been resolved; individual teachers support the type of execution with which they are most familiar, although the proliferation of schools run by ex-members of the New York City Ballet has brought the open-hip position into the mainstream of training.

There is no doubt that the open-hip produces a more attractive line as well as allows a higher extension, but this type of execution needs to be understood within the context of the continuum in training. Just as we do not expect a second-year student to perform multiple *pirouettes* perfectly, we cannot demand from a beginning student a position that will jeopardize placement and alignment. The first years of training are focused on establishing a secure relation between the different parts of the body. Opening out the hip, like turn-out, is a gradual process that begins around the fourth year. This opening out is supported by the squareness of the upper torso (rib cage) and a secure, rotation-free stance on the supporting leg.

Like most other concepts of the classical technique, the open-hip position facilitates motion and enhances line. Only when it is used arbitrarily, without understanding its function, does it become a potentially harmful exaggeration. Two questions should be asked every time the body is pushed beyond its natural range: Is this going to make movement easier? Is the line more attractive because of this positioning?

The course of study that follows is not a named style, but rather a systematic approach based on the traditional precepts of classical ballet, with full acknowledgment of the technical developments of recent years. When formal training begins at age seven or eight, children generally attend one class a week. In the second year, the number of classes increases to two a week, then three for third year students. By age twelve the serious student will be taking a class every day. Also around that age, girls will begin *pointe* work. Some girls may be ready to go on *pointe* by age ten, others may not develop the strength until age thirteen. The time to introduce *pointe* work is a very individual decision.

During the first two or three years, the emphasis of training is less on acquiring vocabulary than on building a strong and correct stance. Much of the classroom time will be spent simply standing in 1st, 2nd, and 3rd positions and in *pointe tendue*. As the well-being and safety of the dancer depend largely on correct alignment fostered in the early years of training and reinforced throughout a dancer's active life, a slow and careful beginning is a most sensible approach.

Although the structure of the class remains the same, after the fourth year the teacher has much more freedom to alter content. Some of the exercises at the barre can be combined and the *enchaînements* in the center can be longer and more complex.

NOTE ON THE LESSONS: TEMPO MARKINGS

Sometimes in fast combinations such as *petit battement sur le cou-de-pied* or *petit allegro* the tempi as marked in these pages can also be played twice as fast while the movement is performed at the slower pace. For example, an exercise marked $\downarrow = 96$ may have music that is played at the faster rate: $\downarrow = 192$.

PART TWO
Lessons

VOCABULARY

Barre	Center
Demi-plié	Stretching
Battement tendu	*Port de bras*
Battement jeté piqué	*Battement tendu*
Rond de jambe par terre	*Pas de bourrée*
Battement frappé	First *arabesque*
Retiré	*Soubresaut, Sauté*
Battement relevé	*Changement*
	Echappé
	Chassé
	Pas de chat
	Temps levé
	Polka
	Grand jeté
	Preparation for turning

FOCUS AND EMPHASIS

The feet are turned out to 45 degrees; children who possess 90-degree turn-out need to be watched in case they roll-in (pronate).

The transition from the freedom of pre-ballet classes to the structure of a regular ballet class may be a little difficult for some children. To ease them into the new discipline, some favorite game or movement can be carried over into this year and performed for a few weeks. It can later be replaced by something that is as much fun but a little more structured. For example, in pre-ballet the children run and leap over a notebook, "jumping over the river." There is no attempt at that time to regulate which leg they kick or if the legs are stretched in the air. In the first year there is more control over the shape of the *jeté* and the steps between the leaps are counted: when done with two steps or runs, the legs in *jeté* alternate; when done with three runs, the leg in *jeté* is always the same, but changes when the movement is repeated from the opposite direction.

The vocabulary for the year is introduced gradually, working from the least difficult to the more complex as the year proceeds.

All movements at the barre are done very slowly to allow time to stretch the knees and point the toes in the extended position as well as to feel the verticality of the body in the closed positions.

Ideally, all exercises should be performed with both hands on the barre, facing the support, but children are easily bored and become distracted when made to stare at a wall. Therefore, holding the barre with one hand, the other in *bras bas* for most exercises, is preferable during this year.

"Hands-on" approach yields the best results initially. The teacher manipulates the limb, placing it gently in the proper position. Later, the child responds to verbal corrections on the basis of the earlier sensation.

Barre

Battements tendus and jetés. Done from 1st position in one sequence to the side only, in the next sequence to the front and the back; later from 3rd position, but only to the side.

Retiré. First practiced from 1st position; later closes in 3rd position, alternately front and back.

Battements relevés. Done *en croix*, initially from 1st position, then from 3rd position. Changing sides should be done formally, with either a *détourné* or little *bourrées*.

Center

Port de bras. First and second are done standing in 1st position *en face*. Each position of the arms is held for several counts before the next position is executed.

Battements tendus. Done to the side only, from 1st position, alternating legs; later from 3rd position, *dessus* and *dessous*.

Arabesque. Introduced from a *dégagé* to the side, arms in 1st position. Turn the body toward the side of the studio, leaving the extended leg behind. Arms extend into first *arabesque* position, the back leg is lifted off the floor. The leg is returned to *pointe tendue*, the body shifts to face front again and the leg closes in 1st position, the arms returning to *bras bas*. This sequence is repeated on the other leg. Later the *arabesque* is preceded by a *chassé en avant*: from 3rd position transfer weight onto the front leg, passing through 4th position; *pointe tendue derrière* with the other leg; lift it into *arabesque*; lower leg and *pas de bourrée dessous*. The arms pass through 1st position during the *chassé*, extend to first *arabesque*, and return to *bras bas* during the *pas de bourrée* when the body returns to *en face*. The sequence is repeated to the other side. This second version cannot be introduced until *pas de bourrée* has been practiced alone.

Allegro. The approach is the same as for the other material: *soubresaut* and *sauté* in 1st and 2nd positions are practiced before *changement* and *échappé* are introduced. *Chassé* from the corner will be done before polka. The arms are held in *bras bas* for the jumps in one place, and 2nd position for traveled jumps like the *grand jeté*.

SAMPLE LESSON
(After three months)

Barre

$\frac{3}{4}$ ♩ = 84

Correct posture is emphasized. This is achieved by holding specific positions for several counts and maintaining the tension in the body throughout a complete exercise, including the closed positions.

Pliés. *Demi-pliés*, three each in 1st, 2nd, and 3rd positions, connected by a *dégagé* to *pointe tendue*.

Counts
1 – 3	Down into *plié*.
4 – 6	Hold position in *demi-plié*.
7 – 9	Straighten knees.
10 – 12	Hold straight position.

Repeat twice more.

1 – 3	*Dégagé* to side, *pointe tendue*.
4 – 6	Hold *pointe tendue*.
7 – 9	Lower heel into 2nd position.
10 – 12	Hold position.

Repeat sequence of *pliés*, *dégagé*, close in 3rd position.
Repeat sequence in 3rd position.

To change sides: Rise on *demi-pointe*, feet in 3rd position, *détourné*. Swivel until the other foot is in front, *bourrée* the rest of the way, finish in 3rd position. *Dégagé* to the side to *pointe tendue*, close in 1st position. Start *demi-pliés* on the opposite side.

$\frac{4}{4}$ ♩ = 80

Battements tendus.   From 1st position, eight *tendus* to the side, arm in *bras bas*.

Counts
1 – 4	*Dégagé* and hold.
5 – 8	Close in 1st position and hold.

To change sides: Close the last *tendu* in 3rd position and *détourné* as above. From 3rd position, eight *tendus* to the side, closing alternately back and front, same counts.

$\frac{2}{4}$ ♩ = 126

Battements jetés piqués.   From 1st position, *dégagé devant* to *pointe tendue*, eight *piqués*, return to 1st position, arm in *bras bas*. Repeat to side, back, and side (*en croix*).

Counts
1 – 2	*Dégagé* to *pointe tendue*.
3 – 6	*Piqués*.

$\frac{3}{4}$ ♩ = 80

7 − 8   Close in 1st position.

1 − 8   Hold 1st position.

Ronds de jambe par terre. From 1st position, four *ronds en dehors*, four *ronds en dedans*, arm in 2nd position. The sequence is followed by a *port de bras* and *cambré* forward, in 1st position.

Counts

1 − 3   *Dégagé* to *pointe tendue devant.*

4 − 6   Circle leg to side.

7 − 9   Circle leg to back.

10 − 12   Return to 1st position.

Repeat three more times.

Reverse sequence, beginning in back. Step away from the barre and face the center of the room. In 1st position, open arms from *bras bas* through 1st position to 2nd position. *Cambré* forward, bringing arms to 5th position as body reaches down. Straighten body, keeping arms in 5th position. Open arms to 2nd position and repeat, same counts.

$\frac{4}{4}$ ♩ = 112

Battements frappés. Preparation, from 3rd position to *cou-de-pied devant* (working heel is placed against the ankle of the supporting leg, toes are flexed and in contact with the floor), arms in *bras bas*. Extend to *pointe tendue* to the side, return to position on *cou-de-pied*. Sixteen *frappés*.

Counts

1 − 2   Extend to *pointe tendue.*

3 − 4   Return to *cou-de-pied.*

Hold last *cou-de-pied* position, bring both arms to 1st position. Hold the position for at least eight counts. Open arms to 2nd position, place heel down into 3rd position, return arms to *bras bas*.

$\frac{3}{4}$ ♩ = 84

Retirés. From 1st position facing the barre, both hands on the barre: lift working heel off the floor, toes flexed and in contact with the floor. Point the toes, only the big toe touches the floor, instep fully stretched. Lift the leg to *demi-jambe* position in front of the supporting leg. Lower leg to 1st position. Repeat three more times. Repeat sequence with the other leg.

Counts

1 − 3   Lift heel.

4 − 6   Point toes.

7 − 9   Lift to *demi-jambe* and hold.

10 − 12   Return to 1st position.

Stretching the hamstrings

Stretching the hamstrings

Turn-out exercise

Leg lifts to the front

Leg lifts to the back

$\frac{4}{4}$ ♩ = 80

Note: Before the end of the year this exercise can be done with one hand on the barre, the other in 2nd position.

Battements relevés. From 1st position, arm in 2nd position, extend working leg to *pointe tendue devant*, lift off the floor to an *en l'air* position, return to *pointe tendue*, close in 1st position. Repeat *en croix*. Initially, the leg lifts to a 45-degree extension, with emphasis on keeping the body vertical as the leg extends up as well as maintaining turn-out. As the student gains these abilities, the height of the extended leg is increased at the teacher's discretion.

Counts
1–4   *Dégagé* to *pointe tendue*.
5–8   Lift leg and hold.
9–12   Lower to *pointe tendue*.
13–16   Close in 1st position and hold. The arm can be lowered to *bras bas*, opened again to 2nd position during the last four counts.

Note: Before the end of the year this exercise can be performed from 3rd position.

Center

The children march to their places in the center in the same manner that they marched to their places at the barre.

Stretching. Splits: front and side, performed slowly, holding the open position about thirty seconds.

Stretching. Hamstrings: legs extended to the front, reach down to touch the toes. Bend legs, chin on knees, gradually stretch out the legs while keeping the chin close to the knees.

Stretching. Turn-out: lying on the back, legs straight, only the heels touching, toes pointed; flex the feet and draw them up, keeping the knees turned out; finish with the toes flexed against the floor and the heels off the floor, thighs fully open; straighten the legs back to beginning position. Repeat four times.

Grands battements. Lying on the back, legs turned out, toes pointed, eight *grands battements* with one leg, eight with the other. Lying on the stomach, hands under the chin, eight *grands battements* to the back with one leg, eight with the other.

$\frac{4}{4}$ ♩ = 56

Port de bras. Standing in 1st position, *en face*, *bras bas*, first *port de bras*: raise arms to 1st position, open to 2nd position, return to *bras bas*.

Counts

1 – 4	Raise on one, hold 1st position for three.
5 – 8	Open to 2nd position on one, hold for three.
9 – 12	Turn palms of the hands downward on one – two; bring arms down on three-four.
13 – 16	Hold *bras bas* position.

Port de bras. Second *port de bras*: raise arms to 1st position, raise to 5th position, open to 2nd position, bring down to *bras bas*.

Counts

1 – 4	Raise to 1st position and hold.
5 – 8	Raise to 5th position and hold.
9 – 12	Open to 2nd position, the palms facing upward as arms lower, turning to face front when 2nd position is reached.
13 – 16	Lower to *bras bas*.

Repeat entire sequence from first *port de bras*.

$\frac{4}{4}$ ♩ = 116

Battements tendus. From 3rd position, right leg back, arms in 2nd position, eight *tendus dessus*, eight *tendus dessous*, legs alternate, head turns toward extended leg with *tendus dessus*, tilts away from extended leg with *tendus dessous*.

Counts

1 – 4	Extend back leg to side, head a quarter turn in that direction (not as far as shoulder).
5 – 8	Close in 3rd position front, head returns to face front.

Repeat with other leg.
Repeat sequence seven more times.
Reverse.

1 – 4	Extend front leg to side, head tilts away from the extended leg.
5 – 8	Close in 3rd position back, head returns to upright position.

Repeat with other leg.
Repeat sequence seven more times.

$\frac{3}{4}$ ♩ = 72

Adagio. From 3rd position, *bras bas*, *chassé en avant* in *effacé* direction, *pointe tendue derrière*, arms in 1st position. Extend arms to first *arabesque* position, lift the leg into *arabesque*. Return to *pointe tendue*. Bring the working leg to *cou-de-pied* position back, *pas de bourrée dessous*. Repeat on other side.

Counts

1–3   *Chassé* forward, transferring weight onto front leg, arms passing from *bras bas* to 1st position. Point back leg in *pointe tendue derrière*.

4–6   Extend arms to first *arabesque* position, head directed toward front arm (the side of the room).

7–9   Lift leg into *arabesque*.

10–12   Hold *arabesque*.

1–3   Lower leg to *pointe tendue derrière*.

4–6   Bring working leg to *cou-de-pied derrière* position, arms in 2nd position, body again facing front.

7–9   *Pas de bourrée*: step onto back leg, step out to side onto other leg, close first leg in 3rd position front; arms return to *bras bas*.

10–12   Hold position.

Repeat on other side.

$\frac{6}{8}$ ♩ = 126

Turning exercise. Hands on hips, feet in almost parallel position on *demi-pointe*, rotate to the right for eight counts with little *bourrées*, leaving the head behind, then whipping it around (spotting). Repeat for eight counts, turning to the left.

$\frac{2}{4}$ ♩ = 84

Allegro. Eight *sautés* in 1st position, eight in 2nd position; sixteen *changements*; arms in *bras bas*.

Counts

1   *Demi-plié*.

2   Jump.

1   Hold *demi-plié* of landing.

2   Jump.

Allegro. Eight *échappés* from 3rd position to 2nd position and back to 3rd position, changing feet, arms held in 2nd position. Counts as for *sautés*.

$\frac{3}{4}$ ♩ = 108

Allegro. From 3rd position, *pas de chat* from one side of the room to the other, arms held in 4th position *devant* (same arm as back leg in 1st position, the other arm in 2nd position).

Counts

1   Raise back leg to *retiré à demi-jambe*, keeping the leg in back.

2   Leap onto the first leg, raising the other to *demi-jambe devant*.

36

3	Close second leg in 3rd position front. Remain on *demi-plié*.
1 – 3	Hold position.

Repeat entire sequence.

$\frac{3}{4}$ $\quad \downarrow = 184$

Allegro. From *pointe tendue croisée derrière*, arms held in 2nd position, *temps levé* from the corner on a diagonal.

Counts

1 – 3	Bring back leg through, step onto it and jump, other leg raised in *demi-jambe derrière*.
1 – 3	Step through and repeat jump.

Note: The music should be a fast waltz.

To finish class, the children return to their positions in the center and stand in 3rd position, *bras bas*.

Révérence. Open front leg to *dégagé* to the side, opening arms to 2nd position. Girls: place working leg in the back and curtsy. Boys: close working leg in an easy 1st position and bow. Repeat with other leg.

SECOND YEAR

VOCABULARY

Barre

Attitude
Retiré passé (to the knee)
Cambré (back)
Grand battement

Center

Grand battement (side)
Port de bras (in 3rd position)
Second *arabesque*
Sous-sus
Balancé
Glissade
Assemblé
Chaînés

FOCUS AND EMPHASIS

The first few lessons of the new year will be spent reviewing the material learned the previous year. The new material can then be added and be fully introduced by midyear.

In view of the inherent logic of the classical ballet technique, no information is ever obsolete. One keeps building, placing concept upon concept, until the full spectrum of the technique is apprehended. All the good habits acquired through the years keep strengthening the foundation of the craft. Progress is measured this year and in all subsequent years by the improvement achieved in the execution of the steps, not merely by how many steps have been added to the vocabulary.

Barre

The barre sequence detailed in the sample lesson will be followed through the year. The exercises are best kept at their simplest, with a few variations described below.

Pliés. Done at the beginning of the year facing the barre, using both hands for support, to emphasize the squareness of the body.

Battements tendus, jetés, and frappés. Performed faster, but a slower tempo can always be used if the execution becomes sloppy. All three of these exercises can be done facing the barre on occasion. A few variations of each may be done. One week, all the *battements tendus* can be performed to the side only; another week, there could be eight *tendus* in each position, or a sequence *en croix* of three *tendus* and a *demi-plié*. For *battements jetés*, the variations can include a preparation for *balancé*: from 1st position, *pointe tendue devant*, lift the leg off the floor, return to *pointe tendue*, close in 1st position; *pointe tendue derriére*, life the leg off the floor, return to *pointe tendue*, close in 1st position; repeat sequence sixteen times. At the end of the *battements frappés* sequence, a balance in *attitude* is performed.

Retiré passé. If done without a *relevé*, one hand on the barre is sufficient; the other is held in 2nd position. Toward the end of the year, performed with a *relevé* and hold on *demi-pointe*, both hands are on the barre for support and squareness. The foot is lifted to the height of the supporting knee.

Grand battement.   Done through the year, with a *dégagé* to *pointe tendue* on the way up and on the return. Change sides with a *détourné*, working leg in 3rd position front, rotation toward the barre. When the working leg is in back at the end of an exercise, as in *attitude*, a *dégagé* is added to bring the leg to the front: stretch the working leg from the *attitude* position to a low 2nd *arabesque*, lower to *pointe tendue derrière*, close in 3rd position back; open working leg to the side to *pointe tendue*, close in 3rd position front. Now the *détourné* can be done.

SAMPLE LESSON
(Middle of the year)

Barre
$\frac{3}{4}$ ♩ = 72

Pliés.   *Demi-pliés*, three each in 1st, 2nd, and 3rd positions. Facing the barre in 1st and 2nd positions; one hand on the barre for 3rd position, other arm in 2nd position.

Counts
1 – 3	Bend knees.
4 – 6	Straighten knees.

Repeat twice more.

1 – 3	Rise on *demi-pointe*.
4 – 6	Lower heels and *dégagé* to 2nd position, placing heel down.

Repeat *pliés* sequence in 2nd position. *Dégagé* to close in 1st position.

Repeat entire sequence once more, executing *dégagé* with other leg.

1 – 3	Turn and place one hand on barre.
4 – 6	Hold position, *bras bas*, feet in 3rd position.
1 – 3	Raise working arm to 1st position, and incline head toward barre.
4 – 6	Open arm to 2nd position, following hand with head; bring head to face front.
1 – 3	Bend knees.
4 – 6	Straighten knees.

Repeat twice more.

1 – 3	*Relevé* and *détourné*.

Repeat sequence on other side.

$\frac{2}{4}$ ♩ = 48

Battements tendus.   From 1st position, facing barre, four *tendus* in each direction *en croix*. With one hand on barre, other arm in 2nd position, eight *tendus* to the side closing alternately back and front.

Counts

1	Extend leg to *pointe tendue* in front.
2	Close in 1st position.

Repeat three more times.

Repeat sequence to side, back, and side.

Repeat entire sequence with other leg.

Turn to place one hand on barre, open other arm to 2nd position; feet in 3rd position.

1	Extend leg side to *pointe tendue*.
2	Close in 3rd position back.
1	Extend leg side to *pointe tendue*.
2	Close in front.

Repeat sequence seven more times.

$\frac{4}{4}$ ♩ = 56

Battements jetés.   The same pattern as for *battements tendus*.

Counts

1	Extend leg to front in *pointe tendue*.
2	Lift toes off floor.
3	Return to *pointe tendue*.
4	Close in 1st position.

Repeat three more times.

Repeat to side, back, and side.

Repeat with other leg.

Note: Instead of the sequence to the side into 3rd position, a series of *piqués* can be executed, arm in 2nd position: eight *piqués* to the front, eight to the side, eight to the back; hold the leg in low *arabesque*; close in 3rd position. Repeat from the back, holding the leg in low *devant* position.

Counts

1	From 3rd position, extend leg to *pointe tendue*.
2 – 8	Lift leg a few inches, bounce toes off floor.
1	Without closing, bring leg to side.
2 – 8	Repeat bouncing action.
1	Bring leg to back.
2 – 8	Repeat bouncing action.
1 – 6	Hold *arabesque*.
7 – 8	Close in 3rd position back.

Repeat sequence in reverse.

Note: The bouncing action should be limited to the working leg, not allowed to affect the stability and placement on the supporting side.

41

$\frac{3}{4}$ ♩ = 80

Ronds de jambe par terre. The same sequence as during the previous year, with a stop in each position, beginning and ending in 1st position. The *port de bras* is done with one hand on the barre and ends with an uplift of the body, the face raised to the arm in 5th position.

Counts for the *port de bras*

1 – 3	Body bends forward as arm moves from 2nd position to 5th position when head is completely down.
4 – 6	Body straightens, arm remains in 5th position.
1 – 3	Uplift in upper body, head turning to look up at raised arm (preparation for *cambré* back).
4 – 6	Body straightens, arm returns to 2nd position.

Repeat once more.

Balance on *demi-pointe*, arms in 5th position, feet in 1st position.

Facing the barre: lift right arm to 5th position, turn head toward arm, bend backward keeping the position, return to upright, replace hand on barre.

Repeat with other arm.

$\frac{4}{4}$ ♩ = 92

Battements frappés. Still to the side, but with an accent out when the leg extends. Additionally, the *cou-de-pied* position alternates from back to front. At the end of sixteen *frappés*, raise working leg to *retiré, passé* into *attitude*.

Counts

1 – 2	From *cou-de-pied* position in front of ankle (toes are flexed and keep contact with floor), extend leg side to *pointe tendue* with strong thrusting-out action.
3	Hold position.
4	Return to *cou-de-pied*, placing heel at back of supporting ankle.

Repeat fifteen more times.

1 – 2	Raise leg to *retiré* position, foot in front of supporting leg, arm in 1st position.
3 – 4	Pass leg to back, lift thigh into *attitude*, arm lifts to 5th position.

Hold *attitude* for several counts. Stretch leg out into *arabesque*, arm opens to 2nd position. Lower leg to *pointe tendue*, close in 3rd position back.

$\frac{3}{4}$ ♩ = 108

Retirés. From 3rd position, facing the barre, a series of three with each leg, the last onto *demi-pointe*. The sequence is repeated with the other leg.

Counts

1 – 3	Raise leg to *retiré*, toes just below supporting knee.
4 – 6	Close leg in 3rd position back.
1 – 3	Raise the leg to *retiré*, bringing toes again to front of supporting leg.
4 – 6	Close in front.
1 – 3	*Demi-plié.*
4 – 6	*Relevé* to *demi-pointe* and bring working leg to *retiré* position.
1 – 3	Hold *relevé.*
4 – 6	Close in back.

Repeat with other leg.

Note: Because the movement always ends closing in back, the students will be moving away from the barre. Before repeating the sequence once more it will be necessary to take a few steps forward, toward the barre.

Battements relevés. As during the previous year, from 3rd position. The *en croix* sequence is repeated twice on the same side. Height is increased, but turn-out and verticality must be strictly monitored.

$\frac{4}{4}$ ♩ = 144

Grands battements. From 3rd position, arm in 2nd position, one *grand battement* in each direction *en croix*. The sequence is repeated twice.

Counts

1	*Dégagé* to *pointe tendue devant*.
2	Lift leg with a throwing quality.
3	Return to *pointe tendue*.
4	Close in 3rd position.

Repeat sequence to side, closing in back.

Repeat to back, and again to side, closing in front.

Repeat entire sequence once more.

Note: Although the students should be encouraged to invest a good deal of energy into the movement, care must be taken that they preserve their placement.

Center

Stretching. Add *grands battements* to the stretches learned and practiced the previous year. Lying on side, arm closest to floor stretched out and head resting on upper arm, other arm placed palm down in front of body to steady position; legs fully stretched, supporting leg's heel lifted off floor and held forward (turned out), toes flexed and pressing into the floor; working leg's heel held next to supporting heel, but toes are stretched.

Counts
1−2   Lift leg as high as it will go.
3−4   Return to starting position.
Repeat seven more times.
Repeat with other leg.

Note: Care must be taken not to roll either forward or back during the leg lift, and to keep the body and the legs in as straight a line as possible.

Stretching.   Side stretches: lying on back, bend knees and bring legs up until thighs are vertical to floor, legs parallel. With tips of toes touching, open thighs out until maximum turn-out is reached, stretch legs out to side, parallel to floor. Bring legs together again, bend knees and repeat stretch.

Counts
1−4   Bring bent legs up to vertical position, knees together.
5−8   Open thighs out.
9−12   Stretch legs out.
1−8   Hold position.
1−4   Bring straight legs together again.
5−8   Bend knees, legs parallel.
9−12   Slide legs down to straight position on floor.
Repeat for a maximum of four times.

Note: Care must be taken to keep the small of the back on the floor when the legs open out.

Stretching.   Back lifts: Lying on stomach, nose on floor, feet stretched out and legs close together, place palms of hands behind neck. Elbows resting on floor throughout, lift upper body off floor without throwing head back. Return to flat position. Repeat movement with hands behind waist, palms up, elbows touching floor.

Counts
1−4   Lift up back.
5−8   Return to flat.
Repeat for a maximum of four times.
Repeat with hands behind waist.

Note: As a final position, the hands can be stretched out

$\frac{4}{4}$ ♩ = 72

Back lifts with hands behind the neck

$\frac{4}{4}$ ♩ = 66

Back lifts with hands behind the waist

$\frac{3}{4}$ ♩ = 69

to the side. The feet must not lift off the floor when the upper body arches up.

Port de bras. Standing in 3rd position, first and second *port de bras. Chassé en avant* to *pointe tendue croisée derrière* with third *port de bras; pas de bourrée dessous*, bringing arms to 2nd position; *sous-sus*, raising arms to 5th position.

Counts

1–3	From *épaulé* position, feet in 3rd position, arms raise to 1st position, head tilts toward back shoulder.
4–6	Arms open to 2nd position, head turns toward front arm.
7–9	Hold position.
10–12	Turn palms down and bring arms to *bras bas*, head remains in turned position.
1–3	Lift arms to 1st position, tilt head.
4–6	Raise arms to 5th position, head turns toward front and tilts slightly up.
7–9	Arms lower to 2nd position, head remains.
10–12	Arms return to *bras bas*, head remains.
1–3	*Chassé en avant* (onto front leg) and *pointe tendue derrière*, arms lift to 1st position, head tilts toward back shoulder.
4–6	Holding *pointe tendue* position, arms to 3rd position (upstage arm in 5th position, downstage arm stays in 1st position).
7–9	Arms to 4th position (downstage arm opens to 2nd position, upstage arm remains in 5th position).
10–12	Back leg comes to *cou-de-pied derrière* position, supporting leg in *demi-plié*, arms open to 2nd position.
1–3	*Pas de bourrée dessous*, end in 3rd position, both legs in *demi-plié* (other leg is now in front), arms lower to *bras bas*.
4–6	*Sous-sus*, arms raised to 5th position, head turned toward front shoulder.
7–9	Return to 3rd position, both heels on floor, arms lower to *bras bas*.
10–12	Hold *épaulé* position.

Repeat entire sequence on other side.

$\frac{4}{4}$ ♩ = 120

Battements tendus. *Battements dessus* and *dessous* as in the previous year, but at a slightly faster tempo.

Counts

1–2   From 3rd position, arms in 2nd position, back leg opens side to *pointe tendue*, head turns toward working leg.

3–4   Working leg closes in front, head returns to face front.

Repeat with other leg.

Repeat sequence seven more times.

Reverse: front leg opens to side, head tilts away from working leg, and working leg closes in back.

$\frac{4}{4}$ ♩ = 76

Adagio. *Chassé* into first *arabesque*, arms change to second *arabesque, pas de bourrée dessous*. Repeat on other side.

Counts

1–4   From 3rd position, *chassé en avant* in *effacé* direction to *pointe tendue derrière*, arms in 1st position.

5–8   Arms to first *arabesque* position (upstage arm *allongé devant*, downstage arm *allongé* in second); working leg lifts into *arabesque*, head looks straight ahead, over front arm toward side of room.

1–4   Arms meet in 1st position, open to second *arabesque* (downstage arm in *allongé devant*, upstage arm in second *allongé*), head turns to look over front shoulder, leg remains in place.

5   Bring working leg to *cou-de-pied derrière* position, body turns to face front, arms in 2nd position.

6–8   *Pas de bourrée dessous*, end in 3rd position, other leg in front.

Repeat on other side.

$\frac{3}{4}$ ♩ = 96

Balancé. This is the simplest *balancé*, the body facing front. The "rocking" action is side to side, weight alternating from one leg to the other.

Counts

1   From 3rd position, open front leg side in low *en l'air* position, arms from 2nd position to 4th position *devant* (opposite arm to supporting leg in 1st position, other in 2nd position), step onto opened leg in *demi-plié*, other leg to *demi-jambe derrière* position.

2	Leg in *demi-jambe* takes weight on *demi-pointe*, other leg stretches out in front, arms remain.
3	Step again onto first leg, arms remain.

Repeat count 1, starting with back (free) leg.

Repeat counts 2 and 3.

Repeat again on other side.

Note: The arms change as the first step of each three counts occurs.

$\frac{2}{4}$ ♩ = 96

Allegro. Four *changements* and two *échappés*. Arms remain in *bras bas*.

Counts

1	From third position, jump and land, bringing other leg in front.
2	Hold *plié*.

Repeat three more times.

1	Jump and land in 2nd position *demi-plié*.
2	Hold *demi-plié*.
1	Jump and land in 3rd position, bringing second leg in front.
2	Hold *demi-plié*.

Repeat once more.

Repeat entire sequence.

$\frac{2}{8}$ ♪ = 116

Allegro. Seven *glissades*, one *changement*. Executed from side to side. The *glissades* are all *sans changer* (without changing feet), back leg starts movement and remains in back. Arms remain in 2nd position through *glissades*, to *bras bas* with *changement*, open again to 2nd position for repeat on other side.

Counts

1	From 3rd position, extend back leg to side, other leg in *demi plié*; transfer weight onto first leg and *demi-plié* on it, other leg extended in *pointe tendue*.
2	Close second leg in front.

Repeat six more times.

1	Jump, changing feet in air.
2	Hold 3rd position.

Repeat sequence on other side.

$\frac{6}{8}$ ♩. = 66

Allegro. Eight *assemblés dessus* and eight *assemblés dessous*, arms remain in 2nd position.

Counts

1   *Dessus*: from 3rd position, open back leg side to low *en l'air* position, other leg in *demi-plié*.

2   Push off supporting leg, land with working leg in 3rd position front.

3   Hold 3rd position in *demi-plié*.

Repeat with other leg.

Repeat sequence seven more times.

Reverse (*dessous*): open front leg, jump and close in back.

$\frac{3}{4}$ ♩ = 176

Allegro.   *Temps levé* in *arabesque* from the corner. The beginning position is *dégagé croisé derrière*, first step is onto working leg. Arms alternate in second *arabesque* position.

Counts

1–2   Step forward and jump, back leg extended in low *arabesque*.

3   Land on front leg.

1–3   Step through with back leg and repeat.

$\frac{6}{8}$ ♩. = 116

Allegro.   *Chaînés*, from one side of the room to the other, arms on hips. At this level these turns are performed in a small 2nd position. Starting with working leg in *pointe tendue devant*, leg opens and steps to side, body swivels a half turn, weight is transferred to other leg; swivel round again, transferring weight onto original leg. The head always spots.

Counts

1   Step onto first leg, head turns to look over leading shoulder (body facing front, head in profile).

2   Step onto second leg, swiveling body a half turn, head turns to look over second shoulder (body is facing upstage, head still turned in original direction).

1   Step onto first leg, swiveling a half turn, head snaps around to look over first shoulder again. Keep swiveling by half turns across room.

Repeat on other side.

Révérence.

THIRD YEAR

VOCABULARY

Barre

Grand plié
Rond de jambe par terre
  (pause in 1st position)
Grand port de bras
Battement frappé en croix
Rond de jambe en l'air
Développé
Petit battement sur le
  cou-de-pied
Stretching with leg on the
  barre

Center

Stretching
Temps liés
Retiré passé with *relevé*
Pirouettes
Détourné
Second *arabesque croisée*
Petit jeté
Entrechat-quatre
Royale

FOCUS AND EMPHASIS

During the third year of study, the subtleties of the classical training begin to be addressed. Corrections will be more probing and awareness of correct line will become a part of the measure of progress. Again there is a period of review before the new material for the year is introduced.

Coordination between arms and legs is emphasized, both at the barre and during the adagio section in the center. Another emphasis is on the upper body. The positioning of the arms in 2nd position is central to the correct development of muscles of the torso. The shoulders should remain down, the shoulder blades flat against the back and not contracted either downward or toward each other; in other words a natural, upright stance is encouraged. When the shoulders are positioned in this manner, the chest can be open and slightly uplifted. From this stance the muscles of the back are engaged and support the arms.

It is a difficult but essential task to make the students understand that it is not necessary to tense the surface muscles, such as the *deltoid* or *biceps*, in order to hold the arms in position. Rather, these muscles need to "lie quietly" on the bones and by this refusal to be activated allow other muscles, such as the *latissimus dorsi* and the *supraspinatus*, to perform the job of holding up the arms. When an untrained person is asked to raise an arm, the movement usually occurs from the shoulder. Ballet training teaches the student to isolate muscular actions, selecting the muscles that can be used most efficiently to perform a specific motion. This process of isolation and selection is the core of learning neuromuscular response.

Barre

Exercises at the barre are essential components of classical dance education. Each exercise conditions and strengthens a specific area of the body; by the end of the barre each major joint (ankle, knee, hip, and shoulder) has been used in two ways—as a supporter and as a prime mover. As a supporter its strength has been tested; as a prime mover its flexibility or mobility has been explored. Both of these functions are necessary to produce motion. The technique is designed to promote movement, not to inhibit it. Thus, beyond the mechanics, the total benefit of a well-balanced barre includes the fostering of a specific neuromuscular response.

Heel down. As children we did not appreciate the importance of this correction, often perceiving it merely as an impediment to getting quickly from one place to the next. But the action of placing the heel firmly back on the floor each time the working leg returns to a closed position (3rd or 5th) conditions the body for quick weight changes in the execution of *petit allegro*, provides the necessary traction during preparations for *pirouettes*, ensures a safe landing in *grand allegro*, and promotes "clean" execution. The benefits do not stop there. The most important function of placing the heel down is that it provides a release of the muscles at the back of the leg (calf and hamstrings) essential to maintaining a healthy musculature. Thirty years ago, when I was a young student, problems with the Achilles' tendon and tendonitis were not common ailments among dancers. If this basic habit is fostered early in training, these ailments can be totally avoided.

Turn-out. The enforcement of turning out correctly— from the hip joint—needs to be closely supervised at the barre. In this year, turn-out can be increased, but not yet stressed if the knees are not completely straight or if there is pronation. Avoidance of "tucking-under" during *grand plié* and during extension, such as *développé*, is one way of promoting correct turn-out.

Center

Temps liés introduce the concepts of weight transference, the oppositional use of arms, and coordination between arms and legs. The adagio can be longer and more complex, and the allegro *enchaînements* can use two or three steps within one combination.

SAMPLE LESSON
(Middle of the year)

Barre
$\frac{4}{4}$ ♩ = 58

Pliés. Facing the barre, *demi-pliés* and *grands pliés* in 1st, 2nd, and 3rd positions.

Counts
1—2   Starting in 1st position, *demi-plié*.
3—4   Straighten knees.
5—6   Rise to *demi-pointe* and hold.
7—8   Bring heels down to floor.
1—4   Descend into *grand plié*, passing carefully through *demi-plié* with heels firmly on floor before allowing heels to rise.

5–8   Rise out of *plié*, again passing through *demi-plié*. Extend right leg side to *pointe tendue* and place heel down in 2nd position.

Repeat sequence in 2nd position. Close right foot 3rd position front.

Repeat sequence in 3rd position. Change to left foot in front.

Repeat in 3rd position.

$\frac{2}{4}$ $\quad \downarrow = 69$

Battements tendus.   Eight *tendus* in each direction *en croix*, the first four with arm held in 2nd position, the last four with arm in 5th position for *tendus* front, in 2nd position for side, and in *allongé devant* for back.

Counts

1   Extend to *pointe tendue devant*.

2   Close in 3rd position.

Repeat three more times.

1   Extend to *pointe tendue devant* and bring arm down through *bras bas* to 5th position, head looking up to uplifted arm.

2   Close in 3rd position, arm and head remain.

Repeat three more times.

1   Extend side to *pointe tendue*, bring arm down to 2nd position.

2   Close in 3rd position front.

Repeat seven more times, closing alternately back and front, the last ending in back.

1   Extend leg to *pointe tendue derrière*.

2   Close in 3rd position.

Repeat three more times.

1   Extend to *pointe tendue derrière* and bring arm down through *bras bas* to 1st position and extend into *allongé*, head turned toward working shoulder.

Repeat three more times, maintaining position of upper body.

1   Extend side to *pointe tendue*, bring arm through rounded 1st position to 2nd.

2   Close in 3rd position back.

Repeat seven more times, alternately closing back and front, the last ending in front.

$\frac{4}{4}$ ♩ = 72

$\frac{3}{4}$ ♩ = 120

Battements jetés. From 3rd position, *en croix*, the arm held in 2nd position.

Counts
1   *Dégagé* to *pointe tendue devant*.
2   Lift toes off floor, raise leg no higher than 45 degrees.
3   Return to *pointe tendue*.
4   Close in 3rd position.
Repeat three more times.
Repeat sequence side, back, and side.

Ronds de jambe par terre. Eight *ronds en dehors*, eight *ronds en dedans*, without a pause except in 1st position. *Grand port de bras* to finish.

Counts
1−3   From 1st position, extend leg to *pointe tendue devant*.
4−6   Circle leg, toes remaining on floor to *pointe tendue derrière*.
7−9   Close in 1st position.
10−12 Hold.
Repeat seven more times.
Repeat sequence *en dedans*, beginning with *pointe tendue derrière* and circling leg to *devant* position.

1−3   *Grand port de bras:* from 1st position, extend working leg to *pointe tendue derrière*.
4−6   *Demi-plié* on supporting leg and place heel of working leg down, deep 4th position, arm in 2nd position.

Counts
1−3   Bend forward over front leg and bring arm up to 5th position.
4−6   Hold position.
1−3   Return body to upright, arm and front leg remain.
4−6   Turn and lift head to look up toward uplifted arm, slightly bend back (upper body only), keeping weight firmly on front leg.
1−3   Return to upright and bring arm to 2nd position.
4−6   Straighten supporting leg, working leg in *pointe tendue derrière*, bring arm to *allongé*

$\frac{2}{4}$ $\quad \math200{J} = 84$

devant and turn head toward working shoulder.

1 – 6   Lift working leg to *arabesque* and balance.

Battements frappés.   Eight *frappés* in each direction *en croix*, *passé* to *attitude* and balance. Preparation: from 3rd position, *degagé* side to *pointe tendue*, bring working foot onto *cou-de-pied devant*; arm opens to 2nd position during the preparation and returns to *bras bas* for the exercise.

Counts

1   Extend leg to *pointe tendue devant* with strong outward thrust.

2   Return to *cou-de-pied* position.

Repeat seven more times.

Repeat sequence to side, back, and side.

1   Raise working foot to *retiré* position in front of supporting knee.

2   Pass through to *attitude*, arm rises through 1st position to 5th position.

Retirés.   Facing barre, two *retirés passés*, *relevé* onto *demi-pointe* and hold. This exercise is especially significant in preparing a foundation for *pirouettes*, which will be introduced in the center. The squareness of the body through the shoulders and hips, the position of the working leg just below the knee of the supporting leg, and the steadiness on the *demi-pointe* need to be emphasized.

$\frac{3}{4}$ $\quad \math200{J} = 100$

Ronds de jambe en l'air.   Introductory version of this exercise. Facing the barre in 3rd position, *rond en l'air en dehors*, *rond en dedans*, repeat each once more, change feet with a *dégagé*, repeat with other leg. The working leg is raised to 90 degrees and the emphasis is on keeping the thigh in place during the movement of the lower leg.

Counts

1 – 3   *Dégagé* side with front leg to *pointe tendue*.

4 – 6   Lift leg to 90 degrees.

7 – 9   Bend leg, bringing toes in to touch back and front of supporting knee, extend to straight position.

10 – 12   Lower leg to *pointe tendue*, close in back.

Repeat *en dedans:* touch front and back of supporting knee, close in front.

Repeat once more *en dehors* and *en dedans*. *Dégagé* to side, close working leg in back.

Repeat sequence on other side.

$\frac{4}{4}$ ♩ = 52

Adagio. One *battement relevé*, *passé* to *retiré* position and *développé, en croix*. At this level, squareness of the hips and turn-out of the working leg are emphasized over height, although students should be able to achieve a good 90-degree extension.

Counts

1−2   From 3rd position, *dégagé* to *pointe tendue devant*, arm in 2nd position.

3−4   Lift leg to 90 degrees and hold.

5−6   Hold position.

7−8   Without lowering, bring leg to *retiré* position, arm through *bras bas* to 1st position.

1−2   *Développé* to *devant*, open arm to 2nd position.

3−4   Hold extension.

5−6   Lower leg to *pointe tendue*.

7−8   Close in 3rd position, arm remains.

Repeat to side, back, and side. Arm is the same for all positions.

$\frac{2}{8}$ ♩ = 84

Petits battements sur le cou-de-pied. At this level, the toes are still kept on the floor, the heel of the working leg touches the supporting ankle alternately front and back. The position of the foot is important in the process of isolating the knee joint, as prime mover, from the hip joint, which is kept still and maintains the turn-out. The lower leg opens just enough to bypass the supporting leg in an even motion, with a slight accent in toward the supporting leg. Preparation: *dégagé* side to *pointe tendue*, open arm to 2nd position; place heel of working foot in front of supporting ankle, toes flexed on floor, lower arm to *bras bas*.

Counts

1   Open slightly to side and strike supporting ankle in back.

2   Open slightly to side and strike supporting ankle in front.

Repeat fifteen more times.

Bring working leg to *retiré* position, rise on *demi-pointe*, raise arm to 1st position; balance.

$\frac{4}{4}$ ♩ = 132

Grands battements. As in the previous year, executed with a *dégagé* to *pointe tendue*, *grand battement*, return to *pointe tendue*, close in 3rd position, arm remains in 2nd position. One *battement en croix*, repeated twice through.

Stretching on the barre. Place working leg on the barre in *seconde*. Bend body toward working leg, opposite arm in 5th position, return to upright; bend away from working leg, other arm in 5th position, return to upright; slide leg along barre, keeping body upright, come back to center; lift leg off barre and hold before closing in 3rd position. (This exercise is performed to a slow adagio tempo.)

Stretching on the floor.   Add the following stretches to the exercises from the previous years: lying on the back, bring one leg up to chest, other straight out on floor; straighten leg and grasp back of calf; pull leg toward the chest; release. Repeat with other leg.

Temps liés.   From 3rd position *épaulé*, *bras bas*. *En avant* and *en arrière*.

Center

$\frac{3}{4}$ ♩ = 126

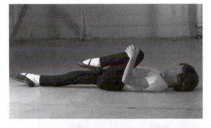

Leg stretches

Counts	
1 – 3	*En avant: chassé en avant* onto front leg, both legs in *demi-plié*, arms rise to 1st position.
4 – 6	Stretch back leg to *pointe tendue croisée derrière*, weight transferring onto front leg as it straightens, arms open to oppositional 4th position.
7 – 9	Hold position.
10 – 12	Close back leg and *demi-plié*, arms remain.
1 – 3	*Chassé* with front leg to side, weight on both legs in 2nd position *demi-plié*, uplifted arm lowers to 1st position, other arm remains in 2nd position.
4 – 6	Straighten supporting leg (leg that initiated *chassé*), other leg to *pointe tendue à la seconde*, arm opens to 2nd position.
7 – 9	Hold position.
10 – 12	Close working leg in front. Repeat sequence on other side.

Repeat entire sequence once more.

Note: In *temps liés en avant*, the *chassé* is always initiated by the front leg, and the final closing from the side is always in front. By contrast, *temps liés en arrière* is begun by the back leg, and the final closing from the side is in the back.

Counts	
1 – 3	*En arrière: chassé* back onto back leg, arms in 1st position.
4 – 6	Front leg extends to *pointe tendue croisée devant*, arms in oppositional 4th position.

7 – 9   Hold position.

10 – 12   Close in front.

1 – 3   *Chassé* with back leg to side, uplifted arm lowers to 1st position.

4 – 6   Straighten supporting leg, *pointe tendue à la seconde* with other leg, open arm to 2nd position.

7 – 9   Hold position.

10 – 12   Close working leg in back.

Repeat to other side.

Repeat entire sequence.

Battements tendus. As in the previous year, *dessus* and *dessous* with the appropriate head movements.

$\frac{4}{4}$ $\quad \downarrow$ = 112

Pirouettes. From 3rd position, working leg in front, arms in 4th position *devant* (same arm as front leg in 1st position, other arm in 2nd position), a series of quarter, half, then one full turns are executed. Preparation: *retiré* to *demi-jambe* with front leg (without rising on *demi-pointe*), close in 3rd position front, both legs in *demi-plié*. During the four quarter turns and the two half turns, the arms stay in their preparatory positions; during the full turn the arms meet in 1st position.

Counts

1   *Retiré* to *demi-jambe.*

2   Close in 3rd position front and *demi-plié* on both legs.

1   *Relevé* at moment of *retiré* and execute quarter turn.

2   Close in front facing next side.

Repeat sequence of preparation and quarter turn until body faces front again (three more times).

Repeat, this time following preparation with half turn (twice).

Repeat, preparation followed by full turn, working leg closing in 3rd position back, arms held in 1st position until closing has occurred, when first arm opens to 2nd position.

Repeat entire sequence on other side.

$\frac{8}{4}$ $\quad \downarrow$ = 58

Adagio. Coordination between arms and head is stressed both during the poses and the transitions. The adagio is still relatively brief, but its components test the ability of the student to retain a sequence. The beginning and end is in 3rd position *épaulé*, the position held until the first movement begins. This sequence consists of a *chassé* into first *arabesque*, *pas de bourrée dessous*, *chassé* in a *croisé* direction into *attitude croisée*, stretch into second *arabesque croisée*, *sous-sus*, *détourné*, and *changement*.

Counts

1 – 2	From 3rd position *épaulé*, *chassé* in *ouverte* direction to *pointe tendue derrière*, arms in 1st position.
3 – 4	Lift leg to *arabesque*, extend arms into *allongé* (first *arabesque*).
5	Hold *arabesque*.
6	*Demi-plié* on supporting leg and bring working leg to *demi-jambe* position *derrière*, body returns to *en face*, arms in 2nd position.
7 – 8	*Pas de bourrée dessous:* step onto back leg, step out into *seconde*, close original working leg in 3rd position front.
1 – 2	*Chassé en avant* in *croisé* direction, stretch back leg to *pointe tendue derrière*, arms are in 1st position.
3 – 4	Lift back leg to *attitude*, arms in oppositional 4th position (opposite arm to front leg in 5th position, other arm in 2nd position).
5	Extend leg to second *arabesque croisée*, arms extend to *allongé* (5th position arm extends *devant*, other arm's palm turns downward).
6	Close leg in 3rd position back, arms in 2nd position.
7	*Sous-sus:* rise on *demi-pointe*, and lower arms to *bras bas*, *détourné*, and raise arms to 5th position.
8	*Demi-plié* on both legs, *changement*, arms remain in 5th position during jump, then open to 2nd position and return to *bras bas*.

Repeat sequence on other side.

$\frac{2}{8}$ ♪ = 152

Allegro. Four *changements*, two *échappés*, arms in *bras bas* during *changements*, pass through 1st position and open to 2nd position during *échappés*.

Counts

1	*Changement*, from 3rd position in *demi-plié* to 3rd position in *demi-plié*.

Repeat three more times.

5	*Echappé*, landing in 2nd position.

6   Return to 3rd position.

Repeat once more.

Repeat sequence four times.

Allegro.   One *glissade*, two *pas de chat*, one *changement*. During *glissade* and *pas de chat*, arms are in 4th position *devant* (same arm as back leg in 1st position, other arm in 2nd position) on the *changement*, arms lower to *bras bas* then open to other side.

Counts
1–3   *Glissade:* from 3rd position, open back leg to side, transfer weight onto it, close the second leg in front.

4–6   *Pas de chat:* lift back leg to *demi-jambe*, push off from supporting leg, land on first leg, other leg in *demi-jambe devant* position, close in front.

7–9   *Pas de chat*.

10–12   *Changement* and hold.

Repeat to other side.

$\frac{2}{8}$ ♩ = 168

Allegro.   *Petit jeté, temps levé*, repeated twice, *assemblé dessus*, arms remain in 2nd position.

Counts
1   *Jeté:* back leg slides out to low *en l'air* position, supporting leg pushes off and assumes *demi-jambe* position *derrière* at moment of landing.

And–2   *Temps levé:* spring up again on same leg.

1   Passing through 3rd position, working leg opens to side and *jeté* is performed on other leg.

And–2   *Temps levé.*

1–2   Passing through 3rd position, working leg opens to side, *assemblé dessus*.

1–2   Hold in 3rd position.

Repeat on other side.

$\frac{4}{4}$ ♩ = 168

Allegro.   *Glissade, grand jeté*, from the corner.

Counts
1–2   From *dégagé* to *pointe tendue croisée derrière*, two running steps, arms from 2nd position through *bras bas* to 1st position.

3   *Grand jeté*, arms assume second *arabesque* position.

Repeat across room (legs alternate in *jetés*).

$\frac{4}{8}$ ♩ = 138

$\frac{4}{4}$ ♩ = 96

Allegro. *Chaînés* from the corner, arms held in 1st position. Preparation: *pointe tendue croisée devant*. The feet during *chaînés* are in a small 2nd position on *demi-pointe*. The body is used as a unit, the arms remain in place.

Allegro. *Petite batterie* (little beats): at the barre, facing and using both hands for support, a series of seven *entrechat-quatre*, one *royale*. Repeat with other leg in front.

Counts

1	*Demi-plié* in 3rd position.
2	Jump, beat back-front, land with same leg in front.

Repeat six more times.

1	*Demi-plié*.
2	Jump, beat front-back.

Repeat on other side.

Révérence.

FOURTH YEAR

VOCABULARY

Barre

5th replaces 3rd position
Cambré back
Battement frappé en croix
Rond de jambe en l'air
  (without pause)
Demi-grand rond de jambe
Grand battement piqué
  Girls (pointe)
Echappé
Sous-sus
Glissade
Pas de bourrée piqué
Assemblé
Piqué to *retiré*
  (Later, in Center)

Center

Grand port de bras
Port de bras en rond
Pirouette en dehors (from
  4th position)
Pirouette en dedans
Pas de basque
Pas de bourrée dessus
Croisé en l'air
Soutenu en tournant
Sissonne
Failli
Assemblé volé
Ballonné
Coupé
  Boys
*Petits sautés à la seconde en
  tournant*
Tour en l'air

FOCUS AND EMPHASIS

Following the initial review period, the vocabulary for the year is introduced gradually. At this age, students begin to appreciate the interrelatedness of the exercises at the barre and the steps in the center. Therefore, many of the corrections at the barre can be made in terms of what will be needed in the center. For example, standing squarely and securely on the supporting leg can be related to *adagio* and *pirouettes*; the execution of *battement jeté*, *frappé* and *grand battement* is applied to the execution of jumps; and *port de bras* can gain a new importance when related to its effect on the performance of *pirouettes* and jumps. Anything that does not directly help execution is going to affect movement negatively.

Because the vocabulary is becoming more extensive it is necessary to continue to stress basic alignment as well as to make sure that transitions between positions, especially of the arms, are correct and clean. The complexity of the technique is founded on the clarity of basic positions and transitions and it is all too easy to be drawn away from these concepts and unconsciously devise shortcuts once the *enchaînements* become more challenging. A solid basic lesson from time to time can serve as a means of keeping these concepts in mind.

Barre

It may seem strange that *cambré* back (full back bend) is not introduced until this year. Most children's backs are supple enough to execute the full bending backward, but it is done mostly by collapsing into the vulnerable waist area. Waiting until the fourth year allows the upper-body musculature to grow in strength in order to sustain and support the backward motion.

Toward the last part of the year, girls will be going on *pointe*. Initially practiced at the barre, ten minutes at the end of the lesson is sufficient. When a good stance is established, the same steps are practiced in the center. To prepare the body to rise on the toes, exercises that foster strength in the ankle and hip joint will be emphasized. Many exercises will be repeated on *demi-pointe*, and some will include *relevés* within the sequence.

The exercises that will be performed on flat foot as well as *demi-pointe* are *battement frappé*, *développé*, *petit battement sur le cou-de-pied*, and *relevé* to *retiré*. *Relevés* can be added to *tendus*, *jetés*, and *ronds de jambe en l'air* combinations. With all rises or balances on *demi-pointe*, attention is directed toward maintaining a strong, balanced verticality on the supporting side. It may even be necessary to perform some exercises facing the barre for extra support, when the *demi-pointe* is initially introduced. In all positions, stress must not be allowed to creep up into the shoulders therefore a straight back and a balanced stance on the supporting hip joint are essential.

Battement tendu en croix. May include a *relevé* in 5th position: three *battements tendus* closing in 5th position, *soussus*. Another version that is beneficial is *battement soutenu*.

Battement jeté en croix. May include a *sissonne* onto *demi-pointe*: two *battements jetés*, *demi-plié* on both legs in 5th position, *relevé* on the supporting leg while the working leg extends to a low *en l'air* position, close in 5th position in *demi-plié*.

Retiré passé with relevé to demi-pointe. May be part of a *rond de jambe en l'air* sequence: two *retirés-passés*, rising on *demi-pointe* and lowering the heel in 5th position, extend the working leg to 90 degrees, two *ronds en l'air en dehors*, close back and repeat *en dedans*.

SAMPLE LESSON
(Latter part of the year)

Barre
3
4 ♩ = 100

Pliés. One *demi-plié*, one *relevé* to *demi-pointe*, one *grand plié*, *cambré* forward and back, in 1st, 2nd, and 5th positions.

Counts
1–3 *Demi-plié* in 1st position, arm in 2nd position.
4–6 Straighten knees.
1–3 *Relevé* to *demi-pointe*.
4–6 Bring heels down.
1–6 *Grand plié*, arm to *bras bas*.

1 – 6	Rising from *grand plié*, arm passes through 1st position and opens again to 2nd position.
1 – 6	*Cambré* forward, arm sweeps to 5th position as bend forward is completed.
1 – 6	Body returns to upright, arm remains.
1 – 6	*Cambré* back, arm remains in 5th position, head straight back.
1 – 6	Body returns to upright; as it rises, arm opens to 2nd position, head turns toward arm. Repeat in 2nd and 5th positions. Balance on *demi-pointe*, feet and arms in 5th position.

$\frac{4}{4}$ ♩ = 60

Battements tendus with battements soutenus.   From 5th position *en croix*: four *tendus*, one soutenu; arm rises to 5th position with each *soutenu* and returns to 2nd position for *tendus*.

Counts

| 1 – 2 | *Tendu* to front. |

Repeat three more times.

1 – 2	*Soutenu*: *dégagé* working leg to *pointe tendue* while supporting leg does *demi-plié*.
3 – 4	As working leg returns to 5th position, rise to *demi-pointe* on both feet; arm lowers through *bras bas* to 5th position.
5 – 6	Hold *demi-pointe* position.
7 – 8	Lower heels down through *demi-plié*, arm opens to 2nd position, straighten knees.

Repeat side, back, and side. Sequence may be repeated once more.

$\frac{2}{4}$ ♩ = 116

Battements jetés.   From 5th position *en croix*: a series of *piqués* followed by four *jetés*; arm remains in 2nd position.

Counts

1 – 2	*Dégagé* to *pointe tendue devant* and lift toes 45 degrees off floor.
3 – 6	*Piqués*: bounce toes off floor four times.
7 – 8	Passing through *pointe tendue*, close in 5th position.
1 – 2	*Battement jeté*.
3 – 8	Three more *jetés*.

Repeat side, back, and side. Sequence may be repeated once more.

65

$\frac{3}{4}$ ♩ = 108

Ronds de jambe par terre.   Preparation: from 5th position, *dégagé* to *pointe tendue devant*, supporting leg in *demi-plié*, arm in 1st position, head inclined toward barre; open leg to 2nd position, supporting leg straightens, arm opens to 2nd position, head follows arm then returns to face front. Four *ronds en dehors*, one *rond* in *demi-plié*; repeat. Repeat sequence twice *en dedans*. The exercise ends with *port de bras* in deep 4th position, *cambré* forward and back, rise from the *plié* to *pointe tendue derrière*, arm *allongé devant*, head looking over shoulder.

Counts

(Two measures of three counts for the preparation.)

1–3   One circling *en dehors*: from *pointe tendue* side, leg circles to back, passes through 1st position, extends to front, circles to side. Repeat continuously three more times.

1–3   *Demi-plié* in first position, working leg stretches to *pointe tendue devant*, arm through *bras bas* to 1st position.

4–6   Working leg circles to side, supporting leg remains in *demi-plié*, arm opens to 2nd position.

7–9   Leg circles to *derrière*, supporting leg still in *demi-plié*, arm remains in 2nd position.

10–12   Supporting leg straightens, working leg in *pointe tendue derrière*.

Repeat entire sequence once more *en dehors*.

Transition: from *pointe tendue derrière*, pass leg through 1st position and extend to *pointe tendue devant*.

Repeat entire sequence *en dedans*: passing through 1st position, leg extends *derrière*, circles to side and front. For *ronds* in *demi-plié*, arm repeats same *port de bras* as for *en dehors*.

Again pass working leg through 1st position from *pointe tendue devant* to *pointe tendue derrière*, *plié* on supporting leg and extend working leg into deep 4th position. The weight of the body remains forward over the front leg during the *port de bras* and *cambré*.

Counts

1–3   *Port de bras* and *cambré:* bend body forward over front leg, arm rises from 2nd position to 5th position.

4 – 6	Straighten body, arm remains.
1 – 3	Bend body back, arm remains, head looks toward arm.
4 – 6	Straighten body, arm opens to 2nd position, head follows movement of arm; rise to *pointe tendue derrière*, arm extended in front.

$\frac{2}{4}$ ♪ = 152

Battements frappés.   Preparation: from 5th position, *dégagé* side to *pointe tendue*, arm opens to 2nd position; place working heel on *cou-de-pied devant* (foot wrapped around ankle). Eight *frappés* in each direction *en croix*, repeated on *demi-pointe*. *Passé* to *attitude* and balance on *demi-pointe* at end of sequence. The arm is held in 2nd position during the *frappés*, passes through 1st position and rises to 5th position for the balance in *attitude*.

Counts

1	Extend leg *devant* a few inches off floor, brushing ball of foot against floor during extension.
2	Replace foot on *cou-de-pied*.

Repeat seven more times.
Repeat side, back, and side.
Repeat entire sequence on *demi-pointe*. (Although the foot still flexes on the *cou-de-pied* position when the exercise is done on *demi-pointe*, the position of the thigh is maintained when the leg extends; therefore, the toes do not brush the floor.)

$\frac{3}{4}$ ♩ = 116

Ronds de jambe en l'air.   Smooth circlings of the lower leg. Two *ronds en dehors*, close 5th position back; two *ronds en dedans*, close 5th position front; two *ronds en dehors*, demi-plié with working leg still extended and *relevé* to *retiré* position to balance, close 5th position back. Repeat, beginning with *ronds en dedans*. Although the working leg closes alternately front and back, the *retiré* position is always in front of the supporting knee. Repeat on *demi-pointe*, rising with extension and coming down in 5th position. The arm is held in 2nd position during the *ronds* and rises to 5th position for the *retiré*.

Counts

1	From 5th position front, extend side to *pointe tendue*.
2 – 3	Lift leg to 90 degrees *en l'air*.
4 – 6	Circle *en dehors* and extend.
7 – 9	Circle and extend.
10	Lower leg to *pointe tendue*.
11 – 12	Close in 5th position back.

Repeat from back with *ronds en dedans*.

Repeat *en dehors*, this time holding leg in extension.

1–3	*Demi-plié* on supporting leg, working leg still extended *en l'air*.
1–3	Bring working leg to *retiré* position and *relevé* to *demi-pointe* on supporting leg, arm through *bras bas* to 5th position for balance.
4–9	Stay on *demi-pointe*.
10–12	Close in 5th position back.

Repeat sequence *en dedans*.

Repeat with rise to *demi-pointe* as leg is lifted to *en l'air* position, supporting heel returns to floor when leg is lowered to *pointe tendue*.

$\frac{4}{4}$ ♩ = 104

Adagio. *Développé* with *demi-grand rond de jambe*. With each *développé*, the arm executes a *port de bras* to 2nd position and remains during the *rond*.

Counts

1–4	*Développé devant*, marking with a slight pause the *cou-de-pied* and the *retiré* positions before extending.
5–8	*Demi-rond* to side; open leg very slowly to arrive on count 8 *à la seconde*.
9–12	Hold.
13–16	Lower leg through *pointe tendue*, close in 5th position front, lower arm to *bras bas*.
1–4	*Développé* side with *port de bras*.
5–8	*Demi-rond* to *derrière*, arm held in 2nd position.
9–12	Hold.
13–16	Lower leg through *pointe tendue*, close in back. Repeat sequence with *développé* back, *demi-rond* side; *développé* side, *demi-rond* front.

Note: Because this exercise is very taxing it is best to perform it on the other side before repeating the sequence on *demi-pointe*. On *demi-pointe* the rise on the supporting leg occurs as the working leg is lifted to *retiré*, and the heel returns to the floor as the working leg lowers to *pointe tendue*.

$\frac{2}{8}$ ♩ = 126

Petits battements sur le cou-de-pied. Sixteen on flat foot, sixteen on *demi-pointe*. The foot is wrapped around the supporting ankle, both on flat and on *demi-pointe*. Arm is held *bras bas* after the initial preparation: from 5th position, *dégagé* side to *pointe tendue*, open arm to 2nd position, place working foot on *cou-de-pied* and lower arm to *bras bas*. The sequence finishes with a balance in *retiré* position, arms in 5th position.

Counts

1   Strike supporting ankle with heel of working leg in back, bypassing supporting leg with a slight opening to side (without straightening working knee).

2   Bypass and strike ankle in front.

Repeat fifteen more times.

Rise on *demi-pointe* and repeat sixteen times.

$\frac{4}{4}$ ♩ = 144

Grands battements.   Two closing in 5th position, one to *pointe tendue*, one from *pointe tendue* to 5th position (*piqué*), *en croix*; arm is held in 2nd position.

Counts

1   From 5th position, kick working leg in front.

2   Close in 5th position front.

Repeat once more.

1   Kick leg.

2   Lower to *pointe tendue*.

1   Kick leg.

2   Close in 5th position front.

Repeat to side, back, and side.

Stretching with leg on the barre.   With leg on barre in front, working arm in 5th position, bend over leg then back; slide along barre to a split position. Repeat with leg to side. Repeat with body turned so that leg is extended back.

Starting with arm in 2nd position, bend body forward, bringing arm to 5th position. Return to upright, keeping arm in 5th position, bend back, open arm to 2nd position as body returns to upright. Repeat. (Do not slide down the barre in the *derrière* position, an action that exerts too much stress on the knee.)

Center

$\frac{3}{4}$ ♩ = 138

Port de bras.   *Pas de basque en avant, port de bras en rond, grand port de bras, pirouettes en dehors* from 4th position, closing in 5th position.

Counts

1–3   *Pas de basque*: from 5th position, *dégagé* to *pointe tendue croisée devant*, supporting leg in *demi-plié*, arms in 1st position.

4–6	*Demi rond par terre à la seconde*, arms open to 2nd position.
7–9	Transfer weight onto extended leg, in *demi-plié*; other leg extends side to *pointe tendue*.
10–12	Bring second leg through 1st position to *chassé* in *croisé* direction *devant*, step onto it, extending other leg to *pointe tendue croisée derrière*; arms pass through *bras bas* (feet in 1st position), open and rise to oppositional 4th position.
1–3	*Port de bras en rond*: bend body forward while bending both knees (back heel replaced on floor), arms remain.
4–6	In a circular motion bring body sideways (toward back leg), and straighten both knees (front leg now in *pointe tendue devant*); 5th position arm has opened to 2nd position, other arm now in 5th position, head turned toward 2nd position arm.
7–9	Continue motion around by bending back, arms remain, head straight back.
10–12	Return to upright, 5th position arm lowers to 2nd position, other arm rises to 5th position, head follows first arm.

Note: The ending for the arms is the same as the beginning, oppositional 4th position, but now the front leg is extended in *pointe tendue devant*.

1–3	Transfer weight to front leg with *demi-plié*, back leg extending in back; sink into deep 4th position, arms remain.
1–3	*Grand port de bras* (action of body and arms is same as in *port de bras en rond*, but weight remains placed on front leg): bend body forward.
4–6	Circular motion to side.
7–12	Circular motion to back; return to upright, arms again in oppositional 4th position.
1–3	Shift weight entirely onto front leg and straighten, extend back leg to *pointe tendue derrière*.
4–6	Place back heel on floor, front leg in *demi-plié*, 5th position arm lowers to 1st position (preparation for *pirouette en dehors*).

1 – 3   *Pirouette.*

4 – 6   Close in 5th position back, arms open to low 2nd position slightly in front of body, palms up.

Repeat sequence to other side.

$\frac{2}{4}$ ♩ = 96

Battements tendus and jetés.   Incorporating *épaulement* positions—*croisé, effacé,* and *écarté*—in a series of two *tendus* and three *jetés,* ending with one *pas de bourrée dessus.*

Counts

1   From 5th position, open front leg to *pointe tendue croisée devant,* arms in oppositional 4th position.

2   Close in 5th position, arms remain.

3 – 4   Repeat *tendu.*

And – 1 Open leg to low *en l'air,* close in 5th position.

Repeat twice more, hold count four.

Repeat sequence in *éffacé* position, arms remain.

Repeat sequence in *écarté devant* position, arms exchange (5th position arm lowers to 2nd position, other arm rises to 5th position), always closing in 5th position front.

1 – 2   Open working leg to side, body *en face,* supporting leg in *demi-plié,* arms in 2nd position.

3 – 4   *Pas de bourrée*: bring working leg into 5th position front and rise on *demi-pointe,* step out to side with other leg.

1   Close original working leg in 5th position back with *demi-plié.*

2 – 4   Hold.

Repeat with other leg.

Repeat entire sequence with *tendus* and *jetés* to back and in *écarté derrière,* same arm remains in 5th position throughout.

$\frac{4}{4}$ ♩ = 108

Battements frappés and petits battements sur le cou-de-pied.   Four *frappés* in *écarté* direction, four counts of *petits battements, tombé en avant* in *croisé, fouetté en dedans,* close in 5th position front.

Counts

And – 1 *Frappé,* arms held in complementary 4th position *devant.* Repeat three more times.

And – 1 *Petit battement*; body turns to *en face,* arms lower to *bras bas.*

Repeat three more times.

71

And – 1 Extend working leg to *croisé devant*, *pointe tendue*.

And – 2 Drop heel to floor in 4th position, front leg in *demi-plié*, arms in complementary 4th position *devant*.

3 – 4 *Fouetté en dedans*: back leg opens to side *en l'air*, then whips into *retiré* position, arms rise to 5th position.

1 Finish turn in 5th position front, arms open to 2nd position.

2 – 4 Hold.

Repeat to other side.

$\frac{4}{4}$ ♩ = 60

Adagio. Traditionally, *grand adagio* in the center starts with *grand plié*. At this level only *grand plié* in 2nd position is performed in the center. *Grand plié* in 2nd position, rise and balance on *demi-pointe*, *dégagé* and close in 5th position front; *développé croisé devant*, *développé croisé derrière* with other leg, *développé à la seconde* with first leg; *soutenu en tournant*.

Counts

1 – 4 *Grand plié* in 2nd position, arms through first *port de bras*.

1 – 2 Rise on *demi-pointe*, arms remain in 2nd position.

3 – 4 Through *demi-plié*, *dégagé* working leg side to *pointe tendue*, close in 5th position front.

1 – 4 Front leg *développé croisé devant*, arms open to oppositional 4th position.

5 – 8 Close, through *pointe tendue*, in 5th position front, arms *bras bas*.

1 – 4 *Développé* back leg to *derrière*, arms pass through 1st position and open to second *arabesque croisée*.

5 – 8 Close, through *pointe tendue*, in 5th position back.

1 – 4 Front leg *développé* side, arms open to 2nd position.

5 Lower leg to *pointe tendue*, *demi-plié* on supporting leg.

6 – 8 *Soutenu*: bring extended leg to 5th position front on *demi-pointe*, swivel toward back leg, back leg coming front; arms from *bras bas* through 1st position to 5th position; *soutenu*

ends on *demi-pointe*, arms in 5th position; bring heels down with *demi-plié*, open front leg to 2nd position.

Repeat on other side.

$\frac{4}{4}$ ♩ = 108

Allegro.   Four *changements*, two *échappés changés*.

Counts

And – 1   Jump and land in 5th position, arms *bras bas*.

Repeat three more times.

And – 1   Jump and land in 2nd position, arms through lst position to 2nd position.

And – 2   Jump and close in 5th position, arms return to *bras bas*. Repeat *échappé* once more.

Repeat sequence.

$\frac{6}{8}$ ♩. = 58

Allegro.   Eight *sissonnes dessus*, eight *sissonnes dessous*.

Counts

1 – And   From 5th position, jump from both feet, arms in 2nd position; open back leg to low side position *en l'air*; land on other leg, uplifted leg closing in 5th position front after landing has occurred, arms in complementary 4th position *devant*, head turned slightly toward forward arm.

Repeat, opening other leg.

Repeat sequence six more times.

Repeat *dessous*: front leg opens side and closes back, arms remain in complementary 4th position at moment of landing.

$\frac{2}{8}$ ♩ = 80

Allegro.   Strength-building enchaînement for boys: one *sissonne ouverte*; one *assemblé* to front, side, and back; two *entrechat-quatre*; arms in 2nd position until *entrechat-quatre*.

Counts

And – 1   From 5th position, jump from both feet, land on back leg, front leg extended in low *devant* position.

And – 2   Jump from supporting leg, land on both feet in 5th position, front leg closing front.

And – 1   Jump, land on back leg, front leg opening side.

And – 2   Jump, land on both feet, working leg closing in 5th position back.

And – 1   Jump, land on front leg, working leg lifted *derrière*.

And – 2 Jump, close in 5th position back.

And – 1 *Entrechat-quatre*, arms lower to *bras bas*.

And – 2 *Entrechat-quatre*.

Repeat on other side.

Note: The *enchaînement* is performed *en face*.

$\frac{2}{8}$ ♩ = 88

Allegro. Three *coupé ballonné dessous*, two *pas de chat*.

Counts

And – 1 From 5th position, *coupé* with back leg, opening other leg to 90 degrees *en l'air* at the same time as push off occurs from *coupé*, arms in 2nd position.

And – 2 Land on *coupé* leg, *ballonné* leg in *retiré* position *derrière*, arms in complementary 4th position *devant*.

Repeat *coupé*, *ballonné* on other leg.

Repeat sequence once more.

And – 1 Without closing back leg (in *retiré*), lift it a little higher with knee still bent, push off other leg for *pas de chat*, arms change from complementary 4th position to oppositional 4th position.

And – 2 Second *pas de chat*.

Repeat sequence on other side. Preparation: pick up back leg.

$\frac{3}{4}$ ♩ = 184

Allegro. From the corner, *failli*, *assemblé volé*, two *balancés*, one *soutenu en tournant*.

Counts

1 – 3 *Failli*: from 5th position *croisé* (right leg in front from the left corner), jump up from both feet, open back leg in low *derriére* position, land on front leg, swing back leg through to 4th position front (*tombé*), arms in 1st position; landing in *croisé*.

1 – 3 *Assemblé volé*: kick back leg in an *écarté devant* direction (body turns), push off from supporting leg, land in 5th position (right leg in front), arms in *allongeé seconde* position, head turned to corner.

Repeat *failli*, *assemblé volé*.

1 – 3 *Balancé*: open front leg, step onto it for three steps that comprise a *balancé*, body turns to

effacé, arms in oppositional 4th position, head looking front.

Repeat *balancé* on other leg.

1 – 3   *Soutenu en tournant:* Open back (right) leg to side, step onto it on *demi-pointe*, bring other leg into 5th position front; swivel around ending with right leg in front; arms lower to *bras bas* during step to side, rise to 5th position during turn; lower heels.

Repeat sequence on same side.

$\frac{2}{4}$ ♩ = 84

Allegro.   *Tours en l'air* for boys. The same sequence as for the introduction of *pirouettes:* by quarter, half, then full turns. Preparation: *sous-sus*, right leg front when turning to the right.

Counts
1 – 2   Working leg in front, *sous-sus*, *demi-plié* same arm as front leg in 1st position, other arm in 2nd position.

3 – 4   Spring up from both legs, arms come to 1st position, execute a quarter turn.

Repeat three more times (full revolution).

Repeat with half turns.

Repeat with one full turn. Front foot remains in front until final turn, when it closes in back.

Repeat sequence on other side.

$\frac{4}{4}$ ♩ = 168

Allegro.   *Petits sautés à la seconde* for boys. Preparation: *pirouette en dehors*, open working leg to side to 90 degrees, arms in 2nd position, body continues to revolve as supporting leg, in *demi-plié*, makes little hops, heel barely off floor, about four hops to every turn. End with *pirouette en dehors*, working leg closes in 4th position back.

Counts
1 – 2   From 5th position, working leg in front, *dégagé* to side and place leg in 4th position back, arms in oppositional 4th position *devant*.

3 – 4   *Pirouette en dehors*, open *à la seconde*, arms in 2nd position, supporting leg in *demi-plié*.

1 – 4   Hop on supporting leg, executing one full revolution.

1 – 4   Continue hopping for another revolution.

1 – 4   Bring working leg to *retiré* as other leg straightens into *relevé* on *demi-pointe*, arms come to 1st

position, finish *pirouette* in 4th position back, arms open to front.

Repeat on other side.

$\frac{4}{4}$ ♩ = 60

Pointe for girls. All exercises are done at the barre, facing the support. *Relevés* in 1st and 2nd positions, rolling up through the feet onto *pointe* and rolling down, eight in each position.

Counts

1−4	Roll up to full *pointe*.
5−8	Roll down.

$\frac{4}{4}$ ♩ = 100

Pointe. Two *sous-sus*, one *échappé* to 2nd position, one *relevé* in 2nd position, close in 5th position, bringing other foot in front.

Counts

1	From 5th position, spring up onto *pointe*.
2	Come down to *demi-plié*.

Repeat.

1	*Echappé* onto *pointe* in 2nd position.
2	*Demi-plié* in 2nd position.
1−2	*Relevé* in 2nd position, close in 5th position, other foot front.

Repeat sequence.

Pointe. Three *glissades sans changer*, one *pas de bourrée dessous*.

Counts

1	From 5th position, open back leg to side, push up onto *pointe*, second leg coming quickly into 5th position front.
2	Hold 5th position on *pointe*.
3	Come down to *demi-plié*.

Repeat twice more.

1	*Pas de bourrée:* raise back leg to *demi-jambe derrière*, step onto it on *pointe*, bring other leg immediately to *demi-jambe devant*.
2	Step onto *pointe* on second leg, raise other leg to *demi-jambe devant*.
3	Come down to 5th position *demi-plié*.

Repeat on other side.

$\frac{4}{4}$ ♩ = 84

Pointe. Four *assemblés dessus*, four *assemblés dessous*.

Counts

1	From 5th position, back leg slides out side to low *en l'air*, other leg in *demi-plié*.
2	Push off from supporting leg, spring up on *pointe*, working leg closes in 5th position front.
3	Hold on *pointe*.
4	Come down to *demi-plié*.

Repeat with other leg.

Repeat sequence once more.

Repeat sequence *assemblé dessous:* front leg working, close in 5th position back on *pointe*.

$\frac{3}{4}$ ♩ = 80

Pointe. A series of *piqués* to *retiré à demi-jambe derrière*. Still with both hands on the barre, but with body angled to allow the *piqué* to be executed forward.

Counts

1	From 5th position, *dégagé* front leg to low *en l'air devant*, other leg in *demi-plié*.
2	Push off back leg, spring up to *pointe* on front leg, back leg in *retiré derrière*.
3	Hold.
1	Come down on back leg in *demi-plié*, extend front leg to *en l'air* position *(coupé)*.
2	*Piqué* onto front leg.
3	Hold.

Repeat sequence six more times.

Repeat on other leg.

Grands battements à la seconde. Eight *dessous*, eight *dessus*.

Révérence.

VOCABULARY

Barre

Plié in 4th position
Battement jeté balancé
Cambré with *pointe tendue devant*
Battement fondu
Grand rond de jambe
Penché
Grand battement en cloche
  Girls *(pointe)*
Echappé to 4th position
Relevé
Jeté sur les pointes
Coupé ballonné
Retiré passé
Soutenu en tournant
  (Later, in Center)

Center

Grand plié in 1st and 5th
  positions
Grande pirouette en attitude
Pas de bourrée en tournant
Temps de cuisse
Sissonne ouverte (with
  développé)
Pas de bourrée couru
Grand jeté en tournant
  Boys *(allegro)*
Assemblé battu
Jeté battu
  Girls *(pointe)*
Pirouette en dehors
Piqué en tournant en dedans

FOCUS AND EMPHASIS

By the fifth year classical placement should be established. The arms and head respond to position of the legs in a "natural" way; correct configurations are performed automatically. Correct alignment is now supported by a stronger musculature. Alignment is not something that a dancer acquires once and for all time. The demands of the training are always slightly ahead of the capability of the student; there is always challenge and alignment is always tested in increasingly complex situations.

At this level, students are both old enough and versed enough in the technique to begin to control and direct their movements consciously. They are able to make increasingly subtle corrections in their execution. This is necessary because extensions are now higher and the demands of *pointe* work have been added, but also heightened awareness of the shape one is making as well as the effort inherent in a motion benefits every aspect of performance.

Barre

Most problems in center exercises arise from incorrect execution at the barre. Stability and mobility in the hip joint are especially important.

Placement of weight. If the weight of the body pulls back or sits on the hip joint, adjustments and compensations are needed to maintain balance in the center, when the support of the barre is no longer available.

Heel down. Failure to put the working heel down affects the execution of jumps in the center. If a student pushes off more from one foot than the other into a jump, the cause lies in the execution of *battements tendu* and *jeté* and *grand battement* at the barre. In all probability, the student is not bearing the weight of the body equally on both feet in starting and closing 5th positions.

Battement fondu. This completes the vocabulary for the barre. *Fondu* is a wonderful composite movement that can be used to illustrate a variety of concepts—alignment on the supporting side; awareness of mobility and placement in the working hip joint; maintaining turn-out of the working thigh in its motion from and to the *demi-jambe* position; coordination between the two legs, as one unfolds and the other straightens, and the arm, which performs a *port de bras*. After *fondu* has been learned and practiced by itself, it can be combined with other exercises for contrast in qualities: in a sequence with *battement frappé*, the percussive quality of *frappé* is enhanced by the melting, supple use of the leg folding and unfolding in *fondu*; in a sequence with *rond de jambe en l'air*, awareness and control in the hip joint are developed as well as contrast between the circular motion in the knee joint of the *rond* and the gradual, aligned, straightening of the knee in *fondu*.

Combinations. Some exercises can now be performed in conjunction with others: *battement tendu* and *jeté*, *battement frappé* and *fondu*, *battement fondu* and *rond de jambe par terre* and *en l'air*, *battement frappé* and *petit battement sur le cou-de-pied*. Some motions are generally used in combination with specific exercises: *battement jeté balancé* ends a *battement jeté* sequence, *cambré* with *pointe tendue* ends a *rond de jambe par terre* sequence, *penché* is part of an adagio sequence, *grand battement en cloche* is performed with a *grand battement* sequence.

Center

Port de bras. Includes *pirouettes en dehors* and *en dedans* as well as *pas de bourrée en tournant*.

Battement tendu and battement frappé. Includes *pirouettes*.

Adagio. Becomes a little longer and more complex, with balances and *grandes pirouettes en attitude*.

Allegro. By this year the vocabulary has covered all four types of jumps—from two feet to two, two feet to one, one foot to one, and one foot to two—in their elementary form.* The introduction of the remaining vocabulary can proceed as the students gain strength.

Beats. Although these are listed under the boys' vocabulary, they should be practiced also by girls.

*For a complete list, see Anna Paskevska, *Both Sides of the Mirror*, (Princeton, NJ: Dance Horizons/Princeton Book Co., Publ., 1981).

Pointe. All the steps of the vocabulary, with the exception of turns, are first introduced and practiced at the barre. It may be necessary to add fifteen minutes to the lesson in order to have adequate time for *pointe* work, but a special *pointe* class need not be introduced until the sixth year.

SAMPLE LESSON
(Middle of the year)

Barre
4/4 ♩ = 58

Pliés. One *demi-plié*, one rise, one *grand plié*, followed by *cambré* forward and back in 2nd, 1st, 4th, and 5th positions. *Plié* sequences from this year on begin with *pliés* in 2nd position.

Counts (slow)
1–2   *Demi-plié* in 2nd position, arm remains in 2nd position.
3–4   Rise on *demi pointe*.
1–4   *Grand plié*, arm through first *port de bras*.
1–4   *Cambré* forward.
1–4   *Cambré* back.
Repeat in 1st, 4th, and 5th positions. At end of full sequence, rise to *demi-pointe*, arms in 5th position and balance.
Repeat on other side.

4/4 ♩ = 88

Battements tendus. One *battement soutenu* rising on *demi-pointe*, three *tendus*, one *battement jeté* (pausing in *pointe tendue* on the way up and back), *en croix*; arm comes to 5th position with each *soutenu*, held in 2nd position for the *battements*.

Counts
1–2   From 5th position, *soutenu*, slide front leg out to *pointe tendue devant*, supporting leg in *demi-plié*, arm lowers to *bras bas*.
3–4   Close working leg in 5th position, rising on *demi pointe*, arm rises to 5th position.
5–6   Bring heels down with small *demi-plié*, arm open to 2nd position.
7–8   One *tendu devant*.
1–4   Two *tendus devant*.
5–6   *Pointe tendue*, raise foot off floor.
7–8   Return toes to *pointe tendue*, close in 5th position. Repeat side, back, and side.

Note: The *soutenu* to the side closes in back following *devant* sequence; *battements* alternate front and back. Following *derrière* sequence the *soutenu* closes in front.

81

$\frac{2}{4}$ ♩ = 104

Battements jetés. Four *battements jetés en croix*, twice; sixteen *battements balancés*, end with balance in low *arabesque* on *demi-pointe*; arm in 5th position for *jetés devant*, 2nd position for *seconde*, *allongé devant* for *derrière*, remains in 2nd position for *balancés*, and is held in *devant allongé* for the balance.

Counts

And – 1   From 5th position one *battement jeté devant*, arm in 5th position.

Repeat three more times.

Repeat side; first *jeté* closes front, others alternate front and back, arm opens to 2nd position.

Repeat *derrière*, arm lowers to *bras bas* and extends to *allongé* position.

Repeat side.

Repeat sequence once more *en croix*.

1   *Balancé*: open leg to front, arm in 2nd position.

2   Swing leg through 1st position to low *derrière*.

3   Swing through 1st position to front.

Repeat thirteen more times.

Note: The working foot must pass through a clean 1st position between each extension; the height of the leg must not exceed 45 degrees. Hold the last *balancé* in a low *arabesque* position, rising on *demi-pointe*, arm in *allongé devant*.

$\frac{3}{4}$ ♩ = 126

Ronds de jambe par terre. Eight *ronds en dehors*, one *rond* on *demi-plié*, *cambré* forward and back. After *ronds en dehors*, *cambré* is in deep 4th position, working leg in back; after *ronds en dedans*, *cambré* is *pointe tendue devant* position, supporting leg in *demi-plié* when body bends forward and straight when body bends back. Balance at end of sequence is in low *devant* extension, arms in 5th position. Preparation: from 5th position, extend leg to *pointe tendue devant*, supporting leg in *demi-plié*, arm in 1st position; open leg *à la seconde pointe tendue*, arm opens to 2nd position.

Counts

1 – 3   *Rond en dehors.*

Repeat seven more times.

1 – 3   *Demi-plié* on supporting leg as working leg extends front, arm in 1st position.

4 – 6   Open working leg *à la seconde*, remain in *demi-plié*, arm opens to 2nd position.

7—9	Continue circling to *derrière*, remain in *demi-plié*.
1—3	Place working heel on floor in deep 4th position and begin *cambré* forward, bringing arm to 5th position as body bends over front leg.
4—6	Straighten body, arm still in 5th position.
1—3	*Cambré* back, weight firmly on front leg, arm in 5th position.
4—6	Straighten body, arm opens to 2nd position, straighten supporting leg, working leg in *pointe tendue derrière*, circle working leg *à la seconde pointe tendue*.

Repeat sequence in reverse: eight *ronds en dedans*, one *rond* in *demi-plié*, *cambré* forward and back with working leg extended *pointe tendue devant*.

1—3	Supporting leg in *demi-plié*, arm in 2nd position, bend body forward over extended leg, keeping weight over supporting leg, arm comes to 5th position.
4—6	Straighten body, straighten supporting leg, keep arm in 5th position.
1—3	Bend back, arm remains in 5th position, head looks toward arm.
4—6	Return to upright, arm opens to 2nd position.

Note: The entire sequence, from *ronds en dehors*, can be repeated. End with balance.

$\frac{3}{4}$ ♩ = 88

Battements fondus. Series of *fondus en croix*, one in each position: first four from *cou-de-pied* position to *pointe tendue*; next from *demi-jambe* to 45-degree extensions; last with rise to *demi-pointe*, working leg extending to 90 degrees. Sequence ends with *relevé* to *retiré* position, balance, arms in 5th position. Preparation: From 5th position, extend working leg to *pointe tendue à la seconde*, arm opens to 2nd position.

Counts
1—3	*Demi-plié* on supporting leg and bring working leg to *cou-de-pied* position *devant*.
4—6	Unfold and stretch working leg to *pointe tendue devant* and straighten supporting leg, arm opens to 2nd through first *port de bras*.
1—3	Return working leg to *cou-de-pied devant*, *demi-plié* on supporting leg, arm lowers to *bras bas*.

4 – 6	Unfold and stretch working leg to *pointe tendue à la seconde*, straighten supporting leg, arm opens to 2nd position.
1 – 3	Return working leg to *cou-de-pied* position *derrière*, *demi-plié* on supporting leg, arm lowers to *bras bas*.
4 – 6	Unfold working leg to *pointe tendue derrière*, straighten supporting leg, arm opens to 2nd position.
1 – 3	Return working leg to *cou-de-pied derrière*, *demi-plié* on supporting leg, arm lowers to *bras bas*.
4 – 6	Unfold and stretch working leg to *pointe tendue à la seconde*, straighten supporting leg, arm opens to 2nd position. Repeat sequence with working leg coming to *demi-jambe* position when supporting leg is in *demi-plié*, opening to 45-degree extension as supporting leg straightens.

Repeat sequence with rise to *demi-pointe* as leg unfolds. To end: *demi-plié* on supporting leg, working leg still extended *à la seconde*; *relevé* to *demi-pointe* on supporting leg, working leg coming to *retiré* position, arms rise to 5th position for the balance.

$\frac{4}{4}$ ♩ = 112

Battements frappés. Four *frappés* front, side, and back; two *frappés double* side. Reverse, beginning with *frappés* back. Repeat entire sequence on *demi-pointe*. The exercise ends with *fouetté en dehors*, balance in *attitude*. Preparation: from 5th position, *dégagé* side to *pointe tendue*, bring working leg to *cou-de-pied devant* (foot wrapped around ankle), arm opens to 2nd position with *dégagé* and returns to *bras bas* for *frappés*.

Counts

1	*Frappés*: working foot strikes outward to low *en l'air* position *devant*.
And – 2	Return to *cou-de-pied*, strike out again.

Repeat two more times.
Repeat side and back.

And – 1	Beat working heel in back then front of supporting ankle, open to side.
And – 2	Hold.
And – 3	Beat front then back of supporting ankle, open to the side.

And – 4 Hold.

Repeat entire sequence beginning back.

Repeat on *demi-pointe*, beginning again front.

Note: Working foot is still used in a wrapped position when on the *cou-de-pied*.

1	*Fouetté*: raise working leg to *retiré* position, supporting leg remains on *demi-pointe*, arm rises to 1st position.
2	Unfold working leg to 90 degrees *en l'air devant*, supporting leg in *demi-plié*, arm in 1st position.
3	Swing working leg *à la seconde en l'air* (keep same height as extension front), supporting leg remains in *demi-plié*, arm opens to 2nd position with working leg.
And	*Relevé* on supporting leg to *demi-pointe*, bring working leg to *retiré* position, arm to 1st position, let go of barre and execute full turn *en dehors*.
4	Hold position on *demi-pointe* in *retiré*.
1	Raise working leg to *attitude*, working arm rises to 5th position, balance. After balance is over, stretch working leg before closing in 5th position.

$\frac{3}{4}$ ♩ = 144

Ronds de jambe en l'air.   Two *retirés passés*, three *ronds en l'air*, *passé* to *développé devant*, demi-grand rond de jambe *à la seconde*, *piqué*, close in back. Repeat *en dedans*.
Repeat entire exercise on *demi-pointe*.

Counts

1 – 3	From 5th position, arm in 2nd position, *retiré passé*, raise working leg to *retiré*, hold.
4 – 6	Close in 5th position back.

Repeat, closing in front.

1 – 3	Open *à la seconde en l'air* (90 degrees).
4 – 6	*Rond de jambe en dehors*.

Repeat twice more for a total of three *ronds*.

1 – 3	Bring working leg to *retiré* position, arm lowers to *bras bas* and rises to 1st position.
1 – 3	*Développé* leg to *en l'air devant*.
1 – 3	*Demi-grand rond de jambe à la seconde*, arm opens to 2nd position.

1–3   *Piqué*: lower working leg to *pointe tendue* and raise to *en l'air* again.

1–3   Close in 5th position back.

Repeat *en dedans*.

Repeat on *demi-pointe*, rising with the *retiré* and lowering heel in all closings in 5th position.

Note: During the *piqué*, the supporting heel also lowers then returns to *demi-pointe* as the leg is lifted. Although the exercise can be done with a *demi-plié* each time the working leg returns to 5th position, performing the rises without bending the knees is a good strength-building exercise.

Stretch with leg on the barre.   Facing working leg (*devant* position), bend toward leg, *cambré* back, sliding along barre. Repeat with leg to side: bend toward and away, slide into side split. Repeat to back, but omit slide.

$\frac{4}{4}$ ♩ = 72

Adagio.   *Grand rond de jambe en dehors*, *penché* in second *arabesque* position; *grand rond de jambe en dedans*, *cambré* back while working leg is extended in *devant* position. Repeat on other side; repeat on *demi-pointe*.

Counts

1–4   From 5th position, *retiré* and *développé* to *devant* (90 degrees or higher), arm passes through *bras bas* and rises to 1st position.

5–8   *Rond de jambe*: carry leg through *seconde* to *derrière*, arm opens to 2nd position.

9–12   Bring arm through *bras bas* to *allongé devant*, *penché*, raising leg as body tilts forward.

13–14   Hold.

Return to upright, close in 5th position back, arm returns to 2nd position.

Repeat beginning with *développé* back and *grand rond en dedans*, arm is same during *développé* and *rond*, passes through 1st position and rises to 5th position for *cambré* back.

Note: *Cambré* with the leg *en l'air* is limited to the upper body, the pelvis remains upright throughout the bending.

Repeat on other side.

Repeat on *demi-pointe*.

$\frac{4}{8}$ ♩ = 138

Petits battements sur le cou-de-pied. Four *petits battements sur le cou-de-pied* (foot wrapped around the supporting ankle), eight *petits battements à demi-jambe* (foot fully pointed, only toes touching supporting leg at calf height), *petit développé* to *pointe tendue à la seconde*, supporting leg in *demi-plié*. Repeat twice on flat foot and twice on *demi-pointe*. Preparation: open working leg *à la seconde pointe tendue*, place foot on *cou-de-pied*, arm opens to 2nd position with *dégagé*, returns to *bras bas*.

Counts

1–4	*Sur le cou-de-pied*, beat back and front.
1–8	Foot points and raises to *demi-jambe*, toes beat back and front.
1–4	Open leg to *pointe tendue à la seconde* and *demi-plié* on supporting leg, arm passes through 1st position and opens to 2nd position, head follows motion of arm; return to *cou-de-pied* position *devant*, arm lowers to *bras bas*.

Repeat once more.
Repeat on *demi-pointe*.

$\frac{4}{4}$ ♩ = 96

Grands battements. Four *grands battements* in each direction *en croix,* sixteen *grands battements en cloche,* hold the last extension (in back) and balance.

Counts

And–1	From 5th position, arm in 2nd position, *grand battement devant*.

Repeat three more times.
Repeat side, back, and side. Last *battement* closes in 5th position front.

And–1	*Grand battement* front, raise arm to 5th position.
And–2	Swing leg through 1st position to *grand battement derrière*, lowering arm to *allongé devant*.

Repeat fourteen more times. Hold last position, lengthening *arabesque* into *allongé*.

Center
$\frac{3}{4}$ ♩ = 96

Port de bras. *Temps liés en avant* with *pirouettes en dehors.* Reverse the combination with *temps liés en arrière* and *pirouettes* or *fouettés en dedans*.

Counts

1–3	From 5th position, *temps lié en avant* onto front leg, back leg extended in *pointe tendue croisée,* arms pass through 1st position and open to oppositional 4th position.

4 – 6	Hold position, close on count 6, arms remain in 4th position.
1 – 3	Slide front leg to side, other leg to *pointe tendue seconde*, uplifted arm passes through 1st and *bras bas* positions and opens to 2nd position.
4 – 6	Hold position, close extended leg in 5th position front.
1 – 3	Repeat *temps lié en avant* with second leg, arms to oppositional 4th position.
4 – 6	Hold *pointe tendue derrière* position.
1 – 3	Place back heel on floor, lower uplifted arm to 1st position, *demi-plié* on front leg.
4 – 6	*Pirouettes en dehors*, close in 5th position back.

Repeat to other side.

1 – 3	Reverse: from 5th position, *temps lié en arrière* onto back leg, front leg extended in *pointe tendue devant croisée*, arms in 4th position oppositional.
4 – 6	Hold position, close on count 6.
1 – 3	Slide back leg to side, other leg to *pointe tendue seconde*, uplifted arm passes through 1st and *bras bas* positions and opens to 2nd position.
4 – 6	Hold position, close in 5th position back.
1 – 3	Repeat *temps lié en arrière* with other leg.
4 – 6	Place front heel down and *demi-plié* on front leg, arms to complementary 4th position *devant, fouettés en dedans*.
1 – 3	*Tombé* onto front leg, other leg in *demi-jambe derrière* position, arms open to 2nd position.
4 – 6	*Pas de bourrée en tournant en dehors*, close in 5th position.

Repeat on other side.

$\frac{2}{4}$ ♩ = 100

Battements tendus.   Two in each position: *croisé devant, en face devant, effacé devant, écarté devant, seconde en face, écarté derrière, effacé derrière, en face derrière, croisé derrière;* two *tendus à la seconde en face;* one *relevé* to *retiré* as peparation for *pirouettes; pirouettes en dehors* from 5th position close in 5th position back. Repeat to other side.

Counts

1 – 2	From 5th position, *tendu devant croisé*, arms in oppositional 4th position.

Repeat.

1–2	*Tendu devant en face*, arms in 2nd position.
Repeat.	

1–2	*Tendu effacé devant*, arms in oppositional 4th position.
Repeat.	

1–2	*Tendu écarté devant*, arms in complementary 4th position, close front.
Repeat, close front.	

1–2	*Tendu à la seconde en face*, close front.
Repeat, close back.	

1–2	*Tendu écarté derrière*, arms in oppositional 4th position, close back.
Repeat, close back.	

1–2	*Tendu effacé derrière*, arms in oppositional 4th position.
Repeat.	

1–2	*Tendu derrière en face*, arms in 2nd position.
Repeat.	

1–2	*Tendu derrière croisé*, arms in oppositional 4th position.
Repeat	

1–2	*Tendu à la seconde en face*, arms in 2nd position, close back.
Repeat, close front.	

1–2	*Relevé* to *retiré*, arms in complementary 4th position *devant*.
3–4	*Demi-plié* in 5th position.
1–2	*Pirouettes en dehors*.
3–4	End in 4th position back, both heels on floor, arms open, palms up.
1–2	Extend back leg in *croisé derrière*.
3–4	Close in 5th position.
Repeat on other side.	

$\frac{2}{4}$ ♩ = 104

Battements frappés and petits battements sur le cou-de-pied. From the corner, four *frappés*, four counts of *petits battements*, two *piqués en dedans*, four counts of *chaînés*, end with the working leg on the *cou-de-pied* ready to start sequence to the same side. Preparation: from left corner, standing in *écarté devant* direction, working foot in *pointe* *tendue seconde écartée,* arms in complementary 4th position *devant,* head turned to downstage corner.

Counts

And – 1   Bring working foot to *cou-de-pied* front, extend in *écarté* direction for *frappé,* arms remain.

And – 2   Return to *cou-de-pied* position in back of supporting ankle, extend again.

Repeat twice more.

1 – 4   *Petits battements sur le cou-de-pied,* arms remain.

1 – 2   *Piqué pirouette en dedans: piqué* onto working leg, other leg in *demi-jambe derrière* position, arms in 1st position, turn, end with *coupé* with back leg, extend front leg to start the next *piqué.*

Repeat.

1 – 3   *Piqué* onto front leg to start *chaînés,* three *chaînés.*

4   End last *chaîné* with working foot on *cou-de-pied.*

Repeat entire sequence.

$\frac{4}{4}$ ♩ = 63

Adagio.   *Grand plié* in 5th position, *développé devant croisé,* arm *épaulé; passé* to first *arabesque; promenade en dedans,* end in second *arabesque ouverte; pas de bourrée dessous* to *tombé* into 4th position preparation; *pirouettes* in *attitude en dedans,* end in *croisé; pas de bourrée dessus en tournant; chassé en avant* to *pointe tendue derrière,* arms in 5th position as final pose.

Counts

1 – 4   *Grand plié,* arms first *port de bras.*

5 – 8   Rise on *demi-pointe,* second *port de bras* to 5th position, balance and hold.

1 – 4   *Développé* to *croisé devant,* arms lower through *bras bas* to complementary 4th position.

5 – 8   Hold extension.

1 – 4   *Passé* to first *arabesque,* arms meet in 1st position, open to complementary *allongé.*

5 – 8   Hold *arabesque.*

1 – 4   *Promenade* toward front arm.

5 – 8   End *promenade* by changing arms to second *arabesque;* front arm opens directly to 2nd

position *allongé*, other arm comes to *allongé devant*.

1–4	*Demi-plié* on supporting leg, *pas de bourrée dessous*, *chassé en avant*, arms lower to *bras bas*.
5–8	*Pointe tendue derrière croisée*, both knees straighten, arms in oppositional 4th position.
1–4	Lower back heel, *demi-plié* on front leg, arms to complementary 4th position *devant*.
5–8	*Pirouettes en attitude en dedans*, end in *croisé*.
1–4	Extend back leg into second *arabesque croisé*, *demi-plié* on the supporting leg.
5–8	*Pas de bourrée dessus en tournant*: working leg drops to *pointe tendue seconde*, bring leg to *demi-pointe* and turn *en dedans* with the three steps of the *pas de bourrée*, end in 5th position.
1–4	*Chassé en avant* to *pointe tendue derrière croisée*, arms in 1st position, rise to 5th position.
5–8	Hold final pose.

Repeat to other side.

$\frac{4}{4}$ ♩ = 104

Allegro. Two *petits jetés dessus* with *temps levé*, *temps de cuisses*, two *sissonnes de côté sans changer*. Boys do *jetés battus*.

Counts

1	From 5th position, *petit jeté dessus*, arms in complementary 4th position *devant*.
And–2	*Temps levé*, arms remain.
1	*Petit jeté* with other leg, other arm comes to *devant*.
And–2	*Temps levé*.
And–1	*Temps de cuisses*: begin movement with *passé*, end in 5th position front in *demi-plié*, other arm comes to *devant*.
And–2	End *temps de cuisses* with small *sissonne*, arms remain.
1	*Sissonne sans changer*.
2	*Sissonne sans changer*, arms remain.

Repeat to other side.

$\frac{3}{4}$ ♩ = 192

Allegro. From the corner on a diagonal, *sissonne ouverte*, *temps levé-tombé*, *glissade*, *assemblé dessus*. Boys do *assemblé battu*. Preparation: from left corner, 5th position, right foot front.

Counts

And – 3 *Sissonne ouverte*: jump up and *développé* back leg, body in *effacé*, arms in oppositional 4th position.

And – 3 *Temps levé* in *arabesque* and *tombé*, passing back leg to 4th position *croisé devant*, *demi-plié* on front leg, uplifted arm opens to 2nd position.

And – 3 *Glissade dessous sans changer*, arms lower to *bras bas*.

And – 3 *Assemblé* in *écarté*, arms open to 2nd position *allongée*, head turned to downstage corner.

Repeat on same side.

$\frac{3}{4}$ ♩ = 176

Allegro.   From downstage corner on a diagonal upstage, *pas de bourrée couru, grand jeté en tournant*, arms do second *port de bras*.

Counts

1 – 3 From *pointe tendue derrière croisée*, arms in second *arabesque* position, three steps upstage, turning toward upstage corner on second step.

4 – 6 *Grand jeté en tournant*: kick original supporting leg to front while other leg pushes off, second leg passes the first leg in the air while body turns in the air to face front again, land in *arabesque croisée*, arms open from 5th position to 2nd position.

Repeat.

$\frac{3}{4}$ ♩ = 168

Allegro.   For boys, preceding *enchaînement* can start with *chassé* and *tours en l'air*, end with *grand jeté en tournant*. Preparation: from upstage left corner, left leg front.

Counts

1 – 3 *Temps levé* and *chassé* forward, back leg passes through *demi-jambe* position and slides forward to 4th position, arms in oppositional 4th position *devant*.

Repeat with other leg, bring other arm in front.

1 – 3 *Assemblé fermé*: raise working right leg to *retiré* with jump, close in 5th position front, arm remains.

1 – 3 *Tours en l'air en dehors*, front leg slips back during turn, close in 5th position back.

Repeat to same side.

$\frac{2}{4}$ ♩ = 104

Pointe (barre).   *Echappé and relevé:* facing barre from 5th position, four *échappés* to 2nd position, close in 5th position alternating legs, one more *échappé*, bring heels down in 2nd position; two *relevés* in 2nd position, one *relevé*, bring feet back to 5th position, and repeat.

Counts

1	Spring up onto *pointe* as legs open to 2nd position.
2	Close in 5th position in *demi-plié*.

Repeat three more times.

1	Spring up onto *pointe* as legs open to 2nd position.
2	Lower to 2nd position, *demi-plié*.
3	Spring up onto *pointe* again.
4	Lower to 2nd position, *demi-plié*.

Repeat.

1	Spring up as legs close together in 5th position on *pointe*.
2	*Demi-plié*.

Repeat sequence.

$\frac{4}{4}$ ♩ = 108

Pointe (barre).   *Echappé* and *retiré passé* with one hand on the barre: one *échappé* to 4th position, one *relevé* in 4th position, close in 5th position; one *échappé* to 2nd position, one *relevé*, close in 5th position back; one *échappé* to 4th position, one *relevé*, close 5th position; two *retirés passés*, closing alternately 5th position front and back. Repeat beginning with working leg in back.

Counts

1	From 5th position, working leg in front, arm in 5th position, spring onto *pointe* in 4th position.
2	Lower to 4th position, *demi-plié*.
3	*Relevé* onto *pointe*.
4	Close in 5th position, *demi-plié*.
1	Spring up to 2nd position, arm lowers to 2nd position.
2	*Demi-plié* in 2nd position.
3	*Relevé* in 2nd position.
4	Close in 5th position, *demi-plié*, working foot in back.
1	Spring up to 4th position, working foot in back, arm in *allongé devant*.
2	*Demi-plié* in 4th position.

3	*Relevé* in 4th position.
4	Close in 5th position, *demi-plié*.
1–2	*Retiré passé:* spring up onto *pointe* on the supporting leg, other leg in *retiré* position in front of supporting knee, close in 5th position front, *demi-plié*, arm rises to 5th position.
3–4	Repeat *retiré passé*, working foot remains in front of supporting knee, close in 5th position back, *demi-plié*, arm returns to 2nd position with *demi-plié*.

Repeat sequence, beginning with working foot in back.

$\frac{3}{4}$ ♩ = 138

Pointe (barre). *Jeté, coupé ballonné, relevé, assemblé:* facing the barre, from 5th position, *jeté dessus, coupé ballonné* and *relevé* in the *retiré* position, *assemblé dessus.*

Counts

1–3	From 5th position, open back leg to low *en l'air à la seconde*, spring up onto that leg, place other leg in *demi-jambe derrière*.
1–2	*Coupé* with back leg directly onto *pointe*, open other leg to 90-degree *seconde*.
3	*Ballonné: demi-plié* on supporting leg, bring extended leg to *demi-jambe derrière*.
1–3	Hold position and *relevé* onto *pointe* on supporting leg.
1–3	*Assemblé*: pass working leg through 5th position to low *en l'air à la seconde*, spring up onto both toes as working leg closes in 5th position front.

Repeat on other side.

Note: All three previous *enchaînements* can also be performed in the center. However, attention can be given to placement and correct alignment by teaching them first at the barre.

$\frac{3}{4}$ ♩ = 120

Pointe (center). *Pirouettes en dehors* with *retiré passé* and *soutenu en tournant.*

Counts

1–3	From 5th position, *retiré passé dessous*, close front leg in 5th position back, arms in 4th position *devant* (same arm front as original front leg).

1 – 3	With same working leg, *retiré passé dessus*, close in 5th position front.
1 – 3	*Relevé* to *retiré* position, close again in 5th position front.
1 – 3	*Pirouettes en dehors* from 5th position front, close in 5th position back.
1 – 3	*Soutenu en tournant:* step up onto *pointe* on front leg, bring other leg in 5th position front, swivel, bringing arms to 5th position.
1 – 3	Complete turn.
1 – 3	Hold position on *pointe*, arms remain in 5th position.
1 – 3	*Demi-plié* in 5th position, arms remain.

Repeat on other side.

$\frac{4}{4}$ ♩ = 100

Pointe (from corner). *Piqué en tournant en dedans.* After a series of *piqués* across the room, end with *chaînés*, lower to a final position flat, such as 4th position, supporting leg in back, arms open to the audience palms up. Preparation: *pointe tendu devant croisée*, arms in complementary 4th position *devant.*

Counts

1	Push off with back leg, spring up onto front leg, working leg in *retiré derrière*, immediately revolve, arm to 1st position.

Note: At the moment of the *piqué* the body has turned to face the corner and the arms are in 2nd position, thus the *piqué* is *en avant*.

2	Come down on back leg, front leg extended in low *en l'air* position *devant*, body in *croisé* (the turn takes the body only three-quarters of the way around).
1	Spring up again in the *piqué*.

Continue on diagonal.

Grands battements. From 5th position *à la seconde*, arms in 2nd position, eight *dessus*, eight *dessous*.

$\frac{3}{4}$ ♩ = 84

Port de bras. *En rond*, once on each side.

Counts

1 – 3	From 5th position, *chassé en avant* to *pointe tendue croisée derrière*, arms open to oppositional 4th position through 1st position.

1 – 3	Bend body forward while *demi-plié* on both legs, uplifted arm stays in 5th position, other arm in 2nd position.
1 – 3	Rotate body side (toward back leg), transferring weight onto back leg and pointing front, uplifted arm lowers to 2nd position, other arm rises to 5th position head is turned toward floor.
1 – 3	Continue rotation by bending back, head straight back.
1 – 3	Straighten body, front leg *pointe tendue croisée devant*, change arms (2nd position arm returns to 5th position, other arm opens to 2nd position).
1 – 3	Hold.
1 – 3	*Rond de jambe par terre en dehors*, close in 5th position back, arms lower to *bras bas*.

Repeat sequence to other side.

Révérence.

VOCABULARY

Barre

Grand plié in 4th position
Battements (with weight
transfer) *tendu, jeté,
frappé, fondu, grand*
Passer la jambe
*Fouetté en dehors, en
dedans*
Flic-flac
Développé in *croisé, effacé,
écarté*
Piqué (with *petit battement*)
Grand battement développé
and *enveloppé*

Center

Grand pirouette in *seconde,
arabesque, attitude
devant*
Balancé en tournant
Cabriole
Failli fouetté sauté
Temps de flèche
Pas de ciseaux
Saut de basque en tournant
Entrechat-cinq volé
Emboîté en tournant
Brisé
Entrechat-six
  Boys (allegro)
Sauté in *arabesque*
Rond de jambe sauté
Brisé volé
  Girls (pointe)
Sissonne
Relevé in big poses
Pirouettes in big poses

FOCUS AND EMPHASIS

In the sixth year the teacher has much more freedom to select the material for each lesson. Nevertheless, the task of preserving the essential clarity of the technique is still, and always, a most important factor in devising exercises and *enchaînements*.

Clarity is maintained by remaining within the tenets of the technique and honoring its rules. All too often the rules of the technique are regarded as obstacles to movement, rather than facilitators and enhancers. For example, a clean 5th position—weight divided equally between both feet—provides a secure base from which to jump or turn and ensures a safe and balanced landing.

Similarly, the action of the arms can either enhance or detract from a motion. A *port de bras en dehors*—arms rising from *bras bas*, passing through 1st position, and either rising to 5th position or opening to 2nd position—facilitates the execution of all jumps as it garners impetus. As the landing occurs with the arms still lifted in 5th position, the opening of the arms into 2nd position is slightly delayed. This preserves the illusion that the body is still airborne and ensures that the tension of the body is not released prematurely, which would endanger a balanced landing.

The rule that *en dehors* movements end in back and *en dedans* movements in front is another instance of a rule that evolved from a natural law of motion. Specifically applicable to *pirouettes*, it allows a smooth ending without struggling against the direction of the spin.

These examples illustrate how the classical technique is founded on basic locomotive precepts, but the positions of arms and head also, although less obviously, are designed to maintain equilibrium by allowing the body's weight to be carried on the supporting side. Modern dance masters have based their techniques on the natural flow of motion: Martha Graham on the rhythm of breathing, Doris Humphrey on the principle of fall and recovery, and José Limón on a circularity of motion in which movement generates an impetus that carries the dancer like a surfer riding a wave. Classical ballet, while not explicitly embracing these notions, nevertheless uses them because they are basic to human movement.

Classical ballet is a highly stylized form of expression that requires a tremendous amount of initial subordination of the "natural" physical response. As such it is often called artificial—a series of learned moves that have little to do with pedestrian usages of the body. This idea could not be farther from the truth; the technique is based on the physical laws governing all human movement and evolved out of these possibilities. Like all dance techniques, balletic movement takes into consideration balance, weight distribution and transference, and the role of gravity. It is easier to perform a motion correctly than to force it against all the rules of locomotion.

Barre

Grand plié. 4th position *grand plié* is not performed until this year. A great deal has been said and written about the adverse effects of *pliés* on the knee joints. Of all *grands pliés*, 4th position is the one most difficult to execute correctly—weight distributed evenly over both feet, support in the thighs, turn-out and verticality of the spine strictly maintained. Although the strength required to perform a *grand plié* should not be underestimated, forced turn-out from the feet at an early age has a far more negative effect on the knee joint than the execution of a slow and controlled *plié*.

There was a time when classical dancers did not suffer from ailments in the knee joint, because exaggerations like forced turn-out and overcrossed 5th position were not considered desirable. The current emphasis on stretching all the ligaments of the body, without enough attention to building correspondingly strong muscles to support the stretch, causes dancers to suffer a long list of dance-related injuries, from tendonitis to torn ligaments. We can ensure the health of our students by fostering balanced alignment and devising exercises that will enable them to maintain strength in proportion to the stretch they have achieved. Finally, more is not always better. One *grand plié* in each position and to each side is perfectly adequate to activate the musculature and place the body in a centered stance.

Weight transference. Combinations that use shifts from one foot to the other become a frequent feature. *Battements tendu, jeté, frappé, fondu*, and *grand battement* are suitable exercises. Toward the end of the year *petit battement sur le cou-de-pied* with *piqué en tournant* can also be added.

When first introduced, the shifts of weight can be quite slow to allow time for a clean transference: two *tendus devant* (the second one finishing in *demi-plié*), one *tendu derrière* with the other leg, closing in 5th position on the last count; four *tendus à la seconde*; repeat the sequence, beginning *derrière* with the working leg. The same sequence becomes a little more challenging if done with three *tendus devant*, one *derrière* with the other leg.

Fouettés. Taken from an extension *en l'air* front for *fouettés en dehors*, back for *fouettés en dedans*.

Flic-flac. First performed without a turn. Toward the latter part of the year it is done *en tournant*.

Although the basic structure of the lesson remains unchanged, the way the exercises of the barre are combined into *enchaînements* now depends on the specific and changing needs of the students. Seeing a problem, the teacher can illustrate the correction with a specific *enchaînement* that allows the student to experience the movement again in another context. The choice of combinations at the barre conditions the shape of and provides a focus for the entire lesson. Nevertheless, the lesson plan must not be so rigid that it precludes a shift of focus if it appears necessary, even if it occurs halfway through the barre. Corrections can be incorporated into subsequent combinations at the barre and into *enchaînements* in the center.

Center

It is impossible to perform all the barre exercises in the center within the same lesson. Therefore, choices are made based on the focus of the lesson and the general balance of the class. No single set of muscles should be overworked; no section of the class should be omitted.

Battement fondu and rond de jambe en l'air. Added to the center practice exercises.

Pirouettes. Executed in *retiré* and in the big poses, they are incorporated into most *enchaînements* of center practice as well as the adagio. They can also enchance a *grand allegro enchaînement*.

In *grand allegro* two versions of the same combination can be done, with *pirouettes* for girls and *tours en l'air* for boys: *glissade, temps de flèche*, three times on a diagonal from the upstage corner (from the left corner the right leg starts the *glissade*, the *temps de flèche* ends in *croisé devant*, left leg up);

101

step through into second *arabesque croisée* preparation; *pas de bourrée, grand jeté en tournant* to the upstage corner, three times; *pas de bourrée en tournant en dehors* toward the back leg, end with the right leg in front; *temps levé, tombé, pas de bourrée* to 4th position, *pirouettes en dehors*, end in 4th position, three times; *chaînés* for girls; for boys, the *enchaînement* can finish with the series of two *chassés*, one *assemblé fermé*, and *tour en l'air* described in the Fifth Year Lesson, repeated three times on a diagonal travelling downstage; preparation to 4th position, *pirouettes en dehors* as the final step.

Pointe

Depending on the students' progress it may be necessary at this level to add a *pointe* class once or twice a week in addition to the technique classes.

Pointe classes generally last an hour and follow the same pattern as regular technique classes; exercises at the barre, *port de bras* sequence in the center, followed by *enchaînements* that include movements from the corner or *en manège*.

Steps at the barre include *échappés, sissonnes, retirés, passés, relevés* in high extensions, *piqués, coupés-ballonnés, glissades*, and *pas de bourrées*, which are linked to some of the exercises of the barre, for example, a series of *tendus* and *échappés* performed *en croix*; *battements jetés* and *sissonnes* also executed *en croix*; *ronds de jambe en l'air* and *coupé-ballonné*; *adagio* performed with *relevés, piqués* into the big poses, and balances on *pointe*; *petits battements battus* with *pas de bourrée piqué*; and *glissades* used in a sequence of *grands battements*.

The *pointe* vocabulary is an extension of the technique's vocabulary. All the rules that pertain to the technique are also relevant in *pointe* work. Generally, the steps of the *petit allegro* vocabulary are suitable for execution on *pointe*, but *grand allegro* vocabulary can be executed on *pointe* in the form of *piqués* or *relevés*; *piqué* and *relevé* in *arabesque* or *attitude*, for example, instead of a leap.

During the sixth year of study we can begin explicitly to address the concepts that lead the dancer toward a transcendence of the technique, that is, through acknowledgement of the basic precepts the dancer uses the acquired expertise and transforms it into artistic expression.

Nevertheless, some basic lessons are not out of place from time to time, in order to maintain a grasp on the fundamentals of the technique and provide an opportunity for the students to address questions of alignment and placement, questions a dancer never outgrows.

SAMPLE LESSON
(High intermediate)

Barre
$\frac{4}{4}$ ♩ = 56

Pliés.   One *demi-plié*, one rise to *demi-pointe*, one *grand plié*, one *port de bras en rond*, in 2nd, 1st, 4th, and 5th positions.

Counts

1 – 2	*Demi-plié*, arm in 2nd position.
3 – 4	Rise on *demi-pointe*, arm remains in 2nd position.
1 – 4	*Grand plié*, arm through first *port de bras*.
1 – 6	*Port de bras*: body bends forward, arm rises from 2nd position to 5th position and remains until conclusion of motion; from bend forward, body circles side and back, returns to vertical; head is angled toward floor when body is sideways, follows arm around to look straight back, then toward arm as it lowers to 2nd position.
7 – 8	*Dégagé* to *pointe tendue*, close in 1st position.

Repeat in 1st, 4th, and 5th positions.

$\frac{4}{4}$ ♩ = 100

Battements tendus.   Two *tendus devant*, *demi-plié*, one *tendu derrière* with other leg; four *tendus* to the side. Repeat, beginning in back.

Counts

1 – 2	From 5th position, *tendu devant*, arm in 5th position.
3 – 4	Repeat *tendu*, end in *demi-plié*.
1 – 4	Stretch back leg to *pointe tendue derrière*, arm in *allongé devant*, hold, close in 5th position on count 4.
1 – 8	Four *tendus* side, end with working leg in 5th position back, arm in 2nd position.
1 – 2	*Tendu derrière*, arm in *allongé devant*.
3 – 4	Repeat *tendu*, end in *demi-plié*.
1 – 4	Stretch front leg to *pointe tendue devant*, arm in 5th position, hold, close in 5th position on count 4.
1 – 8	Four *tendus* side, arm in 2nd position, close last one front.

Repeat sequence.

$\frac{4}{4}$ ♩ = 104

Battements jetés. Four *jetés devant,* four *jetés derrière* with other leg, four *jetés* to the side with original working leg, *demi-plié* and *relevé* to *retiré* position. Repeat, beginning to the back.

Counts

And – 1 From 5th position *jeté devant,* arm in 5th posi-tion.

Repeat three more times.

And – 1 *Jeté derrière,* arm in *allongé* devant.
Repeat three more times.

And – 1 *Jeté* side with original working leg, close first *jeté* back.

Repeat three more times, closing alternately back and front.

And – 1 *Demi-plié, relevé* to *retiré,* arm in 5th position.
2 – 3 Hold.
4 Close in 5th position back, arm returns to 2nd position.

Repeat, beginning back.

Note: The working foot in *retiré* is always in front of the supporting leg during the hold.

$\frac{6}{8}$ ♩. = 50

Ronds de jambe par terre. Four *ronds en dehors,* one *passer la jambe.* Repeat twice *en dehors* and twice *en dedans.* The sequence finishes with *grand port de bras* and *cambré* in a deep 4th position, working leg in back; *cambré,* supporting leg *pointe tendue devant.* (For *grand port de bras,* see Third Year; for *cambré* with *pointe tendue devant,* see Fifth Year.) Preparation: from 5th position, *demi-plié* with working leg extended *devant, demi-rond de jambe à la seconde pointe ten-due.*

Counts

1 – 3 *Rond en dehors,* arm in 2nd position.
Repeat smooth circling three more times, end in *pointe tendue derrière.*

1 – 3 *Passer la jambe:* swing leg through 1st position to 90-degree extension *devant,* arm through 1st position to 5th position.
4 – 6 Bring leg to high *retiré* position, arm remains.
7 – 9 Extend leg to high extension *derrière,* arm opens to high 2nd position *allongée,* head turned toward arm.

10 – 12   Lower leg to *pointe tendue*.
Repeat sequence.

To change legs: pass leg through 1st position to *pointe tendue devant*.
Repeat entire sequence *en dedans*.

Note: Arm for *passer la jambe en dedans*: as leg extends to 90 degrees *derrière*, arm rises to high 2nd position *allongeé*, head turned toward arm; as leg extends to *devant* extension, arm rises to 5th position, lowers through 1st position, opens to 2nd position for *ronds en dedans*.

Transition between *cambrés*: after completing *cambré* in deep 4th position, straighten supporting leg, working leg in *pointe tendue derrière*, close in 5th position; *developpé devant* with front (original supporting) leg, lower to *pointe tendue devant*, execute *cambré* forward and back. End sequence with *piqué* into *arabesque*, balance on *demi-pointe*.

$\frac{3}{4}$ $\downarrow$ = 116

Battements fondus.   *Fondu devant, demi-plié* and *demi-grand rond de jambe à la seconde*, transfer weight onto working leg through 5th position, *fondu devant* with other leg, *demi-plié* bringing leg to retiré position, *relevé* on *demi-pointe*. Reverse sequence: *fondu derrière* with original working leg, *demi-grand rond à la seconde, fondu derrière* with other leg, *relevé* in *retiré*. *Fondu à la seconde* with working leg, *demi-grand rond* to *devant, fondu à la seconde* and *demi-grand rond* to *derrière*; *demi-plié* bringing leg to *retiré relevé*; *demi-plié* as working leg extends to *devant en l'air* (preparation for *fouetté*), *fouetté en dehors*, end on *demi-pointe* in *retiré*. Repeat the sequence in reverse, beginning with *fondu derrière*. Arm performs first *port de bras* with each *fondu*. Preparation: *dégagé à la seconde*.

Counts
1 – 6   *Fondu devant*.
1 – 6   *Demi-plié*, carry leg *à la seconde* while straightening supporting leg.
1 – 6   Bring working leg to 5th position *derrière* (*coupé dessous*), *fondu devant* with other leg.
1 – 6   *Demi-plié* bringing working leg to *retiré, relevé*, arm rises to 5th position.

Repeat sequence, beginning back with original working leg.

1 – 6   *Fondu à la seconde.*

1 – 6   *Demi-plié* carry leg to *devant* while straightening supporting leg.

1 – 6   *Fondu à la seconde.*

1 – 6   *Demi-plié,* carry leg to *derrière,* while straightening supporting leg.

1 – 6   *Demi-plié* bringing working leg to *retiré, relevé* to *demi-pointe,* arm rises to 5th position.

1 – 6   *Développé* to *devant, demi-plié* on supporting leg, arm lowers to 1st position.

1 – 6   *Fouetté en dehors.*

1 – 6   Hold *retiré* position.

Repeat entire sequence, beginning back. The final *fouetté* will be *en dedans.*

1 – 6   *Développé derrière,* supporting leg in *demi-plié,* arm open to 2nd position.

1 – 6   *Fouetté en dedans.*

1 – 6   End *attitude devant,* arm in 5th position, hold.

$\frac{2}{4}$ $\quad$ = 90

Battements frappés.   Three *frappés devant, coupé,* three *frappés derrière* with other leg; four *frappés à la seconde; flic-flac en dedans,* end in *seconde.* Reverse, beginning with *frappés derrière,* the *flic-flac* are *en dehors.* Repeat entire sequence on *demi-pointe* and balance in *seconde.* Preparation: from 5th position, *dégagé à la seconde pointe tendue.*

Counts

1   *Frappé devant.*
Repeat twice more.

4   Bring working leg to 5th position, lift other leg to *cou-de-pied derrière (coupé).*

1   *Frappé derrière* with second leg.
Repeat twice more.

4   *Coupé,* placing original working leg on *cou-de-pied devant.*

1   *Frappé à la seconde.*
Repeat three more times.

1 – 4   *Flic-flac en dedans:* brush ball of working foot on floor in front of supporting leg, which rises to low *demi-pointe;* as brush occurs, begin turn toward barre, end brush with fully pointed foot lifted a few inches off floor; without straightening working leg, brush against floor in back of

supporting leg, open to low *seconde*, completing the turn. Final positon is on full *demi-pointe*, working leg in low *seconde*.

Repeat entire sequence, beginning with *frappés* to *derrière* and *flic-flac en dehors:* brush back then front while turning away from barre.

Repeat entire sequence on *demi-pointe*.

$\frac{3}{4}$ ♩ = 126

Ronds de jambe en l'air. Two *ronds en dehors*, *passé* to *développé devant effacé*, supporting leg in *demi-plié*; open *à la seconde*, straightening supporting leg, one *rond double*, close in 5th position back. Repeat *en dedans* with *développé* to *effacé derrière*.

Counts

1 – 3	From 5th position, open leg *à la seconde*, to 90 degrees, arm in 2nd position.
4 – 6	*Rond en dehors*.
7 – 9	*Rond en dehors*.
10 – 12	*Passé* to *retiré*, lower arm to *bras bas*.
1 – 3	*Développé* to *effacé devant*, supporting leg in *demi-plié*, arm open to 2nd position, head turned toward barre.
4 – 6	Hold.
7 – 9	Straighten supporting leg, open working leg *à la seconde*, fast *double rond en dehors*.

Close in 5th position back.

Repeat sequence *en dedans*. In *développé effacé derrière*, arm is in high 2nd position *allongé*, head is turned toward working arm.

Repeat entire sequence on *demi-pointe*.

Stretching with leg on the barre. Working leg in front, bend forward and back, slide into a split. Repeat side and back, without split to the back.

Counts

An adagio in 4/4 or a very slow waltz.

When a barre sequence incorporates as many *développés* and extensions as in this lesson, I substitute stretching for an adagio. The stretching can also incorporate some *développés* if necessary.

$\frac{2}{4}$ ♩ = 132

Petits battements sur le cou-de-pied. Six *petits battements*, *demi-plié* on supporting leg, *piqué en dehors* with a half turn. Repeat on other side. Repeat once more on each side. Repeat entire sequence on *demi-pointe*. Preparation:

107

from *dégagé à la seconde pointe tendue*, bring working leg to *cou-de-pied devant*, arm in *bras bas*.

Counts

1–6	Six *petits battements* back and front.
7	*Demi-plié* on supporting leg.
8	*Piqué* on working leg, bring other leg to *cou-de-pied devant* and turn toward barre, end facing other side.

Repeat on second side.

Repeat once more.

Repeat entire sequence on *demi-pointe*.

$\frac{4}{4}$ ♩ = 92
March

Grands battements.   Two *grands battements*, one *grand battement développé*, one *grand battement enveloppé*, *en croix*, arm remains in 2nd position.

Counts

And–1	From 5th position, *grand battement devant*, close in 5th position.
And–2	*Grand battement*, close in 5th position.
And–3	*Battement développé*: pass through high *retiré*, open leg to extension, close in 5th position.
And–4	*Enveloppé: grand battement*, then bring leg to *retiré*, close in 5th position.

Repeat side, back, side.

Center
$\frac{6}{8}$ ♪ = 144

Port de bras.   *Glissade en avant* in *croisé* direction, arms in 2nd position; *chassé en avant* to *pointe tendue derrière croisée*, arms in oppositional 4th position, close in 5th position. *Glissade de côté* sans changer with front leg, *chassé de côté* with front leg to *pointe tendue* in *seconde*, arms in 2nd position. *Glissade en arrière* in *croisé* direction, arms in 2nd position; *chassé en arrière* to *pointe tendue devant croisée*, arms in oppositional 4th position. *Demi-plié* on supporting leg and *détourné* toward supporting leg, end in *pointe tendue derrière croisée*, supporting leg straight, arms in oppositional 4th position. *Demi-plié* on supporting leg, *rond de jambe par terre* to *effacé devant*, arms in oppositional 4th position, straighten leg. *Demi-plié* on supporting leg and turn to second *arabesque*, working leg remains *pointe tendue*, straighten knee. *Demi-plié* on supporting leg and *pas de bourrée dessous* to *chassé en avant* into *pointe tendue derrière croisée*, arms in complementary 4th position. *Balancé* through 1st position to *devant effacé* in low *en l'air* extension, arms remain. *Balancé* through 1st position to second *arabesque croisée*, rising on *demi-pointe*; lower supporting heel, place working leg in 4th position, arms in oppositional 4th position *devant* (preparation). *Pirouettes en dehors*, close in 5th position. Repeat to other side.

Counts

1–2	From 5th position, *glissade en avant*, arms in 2nd position.
1–2	*Chassé en avant* to *pointe tendue derrière croisée*, arms lower through *bras bas* to oppositional 4th position.
1–2	*Glissade de côté sans changer*: front leg opens side, remains in front when second leg closes in 5th position, arms in 2nd position.
1–2	*Chassé de côté* with front leg, other leg in *pointe tendue seconde*, arms in 2nd position; close in 5th position front.
1–2	*Glissade en arrière*, arms in 2nd position.
1–2	*Chassé en arrière* to *pointe tendue devant croisée*, arms in oppositional 4th position.
1–2	*Demi-plié* on supporting leg.
1–2	*Détourné*: turn toward back leg, working leg ends in *pointe tendue derrière croisée*, arms shift from oppositional 4th position through 2nd position to oppositional 4th position with other arm up; straighten supporting leg.
1–2	*Demi-plié* on supporting leg, *rond de jambe par terre*, working leg ends *effacé devant*, arms change to oppositional 4th position with other arm up; straighten supporting leg.
1–2	*Demi-plié* on supporting leg, shift heel of supporting leg forward and turn body away from working leg into second *arabesque* position, arms in second *arabesque*; straighten supporting leg.
1–2	*Demi-plié* and *pas de bourrée dessous*, end with *chassé en avant* to *pointe tendue derrière croisée*, arms in complementary 4th position.
1–2	*Balancé* to *devant en l'air effacé*, arms remain.
1–2	*Balancé* to second *arabesque croisée*, arms in second *arabesque*, rise on *demi-pointe* as leg rises.
1–2	Drop working leg into 4th position, supporting leg in *demi-plié*, arms in oppositional 4th position *devant*.
1–2	*Pirouettes en dehors*, close in 5th position back.

Repeat to other side.

$\frac{2}{4}$ ♩ = 69

Battements tendus with pirouettes en dedans.   Two *battements tendus dessous*, alternate legs closing in back; two *tendus dessus*, alternate legs closing in front; two *tendus devant* in *effacé*; two *tendus derrière* in *effacé* (with other leg); two *tendus* in *écarté devant* with front leg closing front each time; *relevé* to low *écarté devant* position *en l'air*, *tombé*, *pas de bourrée* to 4th position preparation; *pirouettes en dedans*, end in 4th position, weight on working leg; *pirouettes en dedans* to other side, end in 5th position front. Repeat to other side.

Counts

And – 2	From 5th position, front leg *tendu à la seconde*, close back, arms in 2nd position.
3 – 4	*Tendu dessous* with other leg.
1 – 2	Open back leg *à la seconde*, close in front.
3 – 4	*Tendu dessus* with other leg.
1 – 2	*Tendu devant* in *effacé* with front leg, arms in oppositional 4th position.
3 – 4	Repeat *tendu devant effacé*.
1 – 2	*Tendu derrière* in *effacé* with other leg, arms remain.
3 – 4	Repeat *tendu derrière effacé*.
1 – 2	*Tendu* in *écarté devant* with other leg, arms in complementary 4th position; close front.
3 – 4	Repeat *tendu* in *écarté devant*; close front.
1 – 2	*Relevé* to *demi-pointe* on supporting leg, open front leg to low *en l'air* in *écarté devant*.
3 – 4	*Tombé* onto working leg, *pas de bourrée dessous*, end in 4th position *croisé*, arms in complementary 4th position (preparation).
1 – 2	*Pirouettes en dedans*, end in 4th position, working leg forward, arms in complementary 4th position.
3 – 4	*Pirouettes en dedans*, end in 5th position, working leg front.

Repeat to other side.

$\frac{3}{4}$ ♩ = 132

Ronds de jambe en l'air with grandes pirouettes in attitude en dedans.   Two *balancés en tournant*, one *soutenu en tournant*; two *ronds en l'air en dehors*, *développé devant effacé*, supporting leg in *demi-plié*, return to *seconde*; two *ronds en l'air en dedans*, *développé* to *effacé derrière*, supporting leg in *demi-plié*; *pas de bourrée dessous*, end in 4th position *croisé* (preparation); *pirouettes en dedans* in *attitude*, end in *effacé*; extend working leg to *arabesque*, supporting leg in *demi-plié*; *pas de bourrée dessous*. Repeat to the other side.

Counts

1–3   First *balancé*: from 5th position, open front leg, step onto it on count 1, body turns in same direction, head stays behind, facing front, looking over shoulder and front arm which is in 1st position; continue turning on counts 2 and 3.

4–6   Step onto other leg, body facing other side in profile, other arm in front, head facing front looking over shoulder.

7–9   Open back leg, turn toward it, step onto *demi-pointe*, arms to *bras bas*; *soutenu*: turn toward leg that opened, other leg closes 5th position front on *demi-pointe* (swivel brings first leg front again), arms rise to 5th position during turn.

10–12   Hold 5th position on *demi-pointe*, bring heels down on count 3.

1–3   Open front leg *à la seconde* to 90 degrees, arms in 2nd position.

4–6   *Rond en l'air en dehors.*

7–9   Repeat *rond en dehors.*

10–12   *Passé* through high *retiré*, *développé devant effacé*, supporting leg in *demi-plié*, arms in oppositional 4th position.

1–3   Return *à la seconde* and straighten supporting leg, arms return to 2nd position.

4–6   *Rond en l'air en dedans.*

7–9   Repeat *rond en dedans.*

10–12   *Passé* to *développé derrière effacé*, supporting leg in *demi-plié*, arms in oppositional 4th position.

1–3   *Pas de bourrée dessous*, end in 4th position *croisé*, front leg in *demi-plié*, arms in complementary 4th position *devant*.

4–6   *Pirouettes en dedans* in *attitude*, end in *effacé*, arms in oppositional 4th position.

7–9   Stretch leg into *arabesque effacé*, arms extend into *allongé*.

10–12   *Pas de bourrée dessous*, arms return to *bras bas*.

Repeat on other side.

$\frac{4}{4}$ ♩ = 60

Adagio. *Développés* to *croisé* and *effacé*, *devant* and *derrière*, and *écarté devant* and *derrière*, change legs each time; *piqué en arrière* (onto the *écarté derrière* leg) with small *fouetté* and turn body toward working leg which is in *effacé devant*; *fouetté* with *relevé* to first *arabesque* (preparation); *grand fouetté en tournant*, end in first *arabesque*; *balancé* to *croisé devant* with *relevé*, *tombé* to 4th position *croisé*; *pirouettes* in *arabesque en dedans*; end *pirouettes* by holding first *arabesque*; *lié* (step onto working leg) through to 4th position *croisé*, arms in oppositional 4th position *allongé*, back leg in *pointe tendue croisée derrière*. Repeat on other side.

Counts

1–4	From 5th position, front leg *développé* to *croisé devant*, arms open to oppositional 4th position.
5–6	Hold.
7–8	Close in 5th position with small rise to *demi-pointe*, arms lower to *bras bas*.
1–4	Back leg *développé croisé derrière*, arms lift to complementary 4th position (other leg).
5–6	Hold.
7–8	Close in 5th position with rise to *demi-pointe*, arms lower to *bras bas*.
1–4	Front leg *développé* to *effacé devant*, arms open to oppositional 4th position.
5–6	Hold.
7–8	Close in 5th position front with rise, arms remain.
1–4	Back leg *développé* to *effacé derrière*, arms remain.
5–6	Hold.
7–8	Close in 5th position back with rise, arms lower to *bras bas*.
1–4	Front leg *développé écarté devant*, arms in complementary 4th position.
5–6	Hold.
7–8	Close in 5th position front, arms lower to *bras bas*.
1–4	Back leg *développé écarté derrière*, arms in oppositional 4th position.
5–8	*Fouetté* into first *arabesque* with rise on *demi-pointe* (the leg stays in place while the body turns away), arms in first *arabesque* position.
1–4	*Relevé*, arms open to 2nd position, quick *demi-plié* and *fouetté en tournant*: supporting leg on *demi-pointe*, working leg swings through 1st position to *devant en l'air* while body revolves a three-quarter turn, arms lift to 5th position;

body whips away from leg, leaving leg in first *arabesque*, arms return to *arabesque* position; end with small *demi-plié* on supporting leg.

1–4   *Balancé* through 1st position to *croisé devant* with *relevé* onto *demi-pointe*, arms in oppositional 4th position.

1–4   *Tombé* to *croisé devant*, front leg in *demi-plié*, arms in complementary 4th position *devant* (preparation).

1–4   *Pirouettes en arabesque en dedans*, arms in first *arabesque*, end with small *demi-plié*.

5–8   Hold *arabesque* (supporting knee straight).

1–4   Bring working leg forward through first position, step onto it (*lié*) with small *demi-plié*, back leg in *pointe tendue derrière*, arms in 4th position *devant allongé*.

5–8   Hold. Bring back leg to 5th position front on count 8.

Repeat to other side.

$\frac{2}{4}$ $\quad$ = 100

Allegro. Two *changements*, one *sissonne ordinaire devant*, *assemblé dessous*. Repeat on other side. Two *changements*, one *sissonne ordinaire derrière*, *assemblé dessus*. Repeat on other side. Two *sissonnes de côté dessus*, two *sissonnes de côté dessous*; *soutenu en tournant en dedans*, *changement*. Repeat entire sequence on other side. Arms remain in *bras bas* or low 2nd position.

Counts

And–1 *Changement*.

And–2 *Changement*.

And–3 *Sissonne ordinaire*, front leg ends in *demi-jambe devant*.

And–4 *Assemblé dessous*: working leg passes through 5th position before opening to side, closes in back.

Repeat on other side.

Repeat two *changements*.

And–3 *Sissonne ordinaire derrière*, back leg in *demi-jambe derrière*.

And–4 *Assemblé dessus*: working leg closes in front.

Repeat on other side.

And–1 *Sissonne de côté dessus*: back leg opens to side, closes in front.

Repeat with other leg.

Repeat two *sissonnes dessus*.

And – 3   *Sissonne de côté dessous*: front leg opens to side, closes in back.

Repeat with other leg.

Repeat two *sissonnes dessus*.

And – 1   *Soutenu*: open back leg to side, turn toward supporting leg as working leg closes in 5th position.

And – 4   Hold on *demi-pointe*.

And – 1   *Demi-plié* and 3 *changements*.

And – 4   Hold.

Repeat to other side.

Note: This *enchaînement* can also include beats: *royal* for *changements*, *entrechat-cinq* for *sissonne ordinaire*, *assemblé battu*, and *sissonne battu*.

$\frac{6}{8}$ ♩. = 69

Allegro.   *Failli fouetté sauté, temps levé-tombé, cabriole devant* in *effacé* direction, close in 5th position front. Repeat sequence on other side.

Counts

1 – 3   From 5th position, *failli*: jump off both feet, open back leg slightly *derrière effacé* in air, swing leg through 1st position to 4th position *croisé devant*, weight on front leg in *demi-plié*, other leg straight, heel on floor; arms from 2nd position pass through *bras bas*.

1 – 3   *Fouetté*: back leg brushes through 1st position and lifts to 90 degrees in *devant effacé* direction as push-off occurs; at apex of jump, body turns away from working leg, landing in first *arabesque*; arms rise through 1st position to 5th position, open to first *arabesque* position with landing.

1 – 3   *Temps levé-tombé*: jump up from supporting leg without lowering working leg, swing working leg through 1st position to 4th position *croisé devant*, front leg in *demi-plié*; arms lower to *bras bas*.

1 – 3   *Cabriole*: Swing back leg through 1st position to *effacé devant* as supporting leg pushes off; supporting leg rises to beat back of working leg, propelling it higher; land on back leg, with

working leg still in air, close working leg in 5th position front. Arms in oppositional 4th position until after landing.

Repeat on other side.

$\frac{3}{4}$ ♩ = 96

Allegro. *Tombé pas de ciseaux*, repeated four times on alternate legs; *chassé* into *saut de basque en tournant*, repeated three times; *balancé*. Repeat on other side. This *enchaînement* is best performed to a mazurka.

Counts

1   *Tombé* into 4th position *croisé devant, coupé* with back leg, arms in 1st position.

2–3   Kick front leg as push-off occurs, kick second leg in same direction; legs pass each other in air, end movement on first leg, with second leg extended *en l'air devant*; arms rise to 5th position with push-off, open out with landing.

Repeat three more times.

Note: Both legs kick in a *croisé* direction, thus the body turns subtly from one side to the other as the jump occurs.

1   *Chassé* in an *effacé* direction on a diagonal, arms in 2nd position. Step onto front leg, kick other leg to *croisé devant*, turning body to face corner; supporting leg pushes off at same time, arms rise through 1st position to 5th position.

3   Body rotates in air as leg that pushed off comes to high *retiré* position, land in *retiré*, facing front, arms in 5th position.

Repeat two more times.

1–3   *Tombé* onto working leg to start *balancé*, arms to oppositional 4th position *devant*; end *balancé* on front leg.

Repeat on other side, beginning with back leg.

Note: The *pas de ciseaux* can be replaced by *temps de flèche*.

$\frac{3}{4}$ ♩ = 168

Waltz

Allegro. *Failli, entrechat-cinq* from the corner on a diagonal. *Entrechat-cinq* is an *assemblé volé battu*; the working leg beats front, then back, and front again.

Counts

And–3   From 5th position, *failli* into 4th position *croisé devant*, arms through *bras bas* to 1st position.

115

And – 3 Kick back leg to *écarté devant* position, body turns from *croisé* to *écarté*, arms open to *allongé* in 2nd position, front arm higher than back; beat legs at apex of jump, end in 5th position.

Repeat.

$\frac{2}{4}$ $\quad \downarrow = 160$

Allegro. Two *brisés en avant*, two *brisés en arrière*, one *brisé en avant*, *sous-sus*, *entrechat-six*.

Counts

And – 1 *Brisé en avant*, traveling forward diagonally: from 5th position, open back leg to low *effacé devant*, push off supporting leg, beat back and front of uplifted leg, land in 5th position; arms in oppositional 4th position *devant*, body angled slightly forward and over working leg.

Repeat.

And – 1 *Brisé en arrière*, traveling back diagonally: open front leg to low *effacé derrière* position, push off supporting leg, beat front and back, land in 5th position; arms in complementary 4th position *devant*, back arched.

Repeat.

And – 1 *Brisé en avant*.

And – 2 *Sous-sus: relevé* in 5th position to *demi-pointe*, arms open to 2nd position.

And – 3 *Demi-plié*.

And – 4 *Entrechat-six*, land in 5th position, other leg in front. Repeat to other side.

Five allegro *enchaînements* are generally the limit for jumping combinations in a class. The limitation is imposed by time and the physical stamina of the students. The selection of jumps usually includes a warm-up exercise (e.g., the first allegro in this lesson), followed by a *petit allegro enchaînement* (e.g., the first and second *enchaînements* in the Fifth Year Lesson or the second *enchaînement* in this lesson). Then, a *grand allegro* is executed (e.g., the third and fourth *enchaînements* in this lesson or the third in the Fifth Year Lesson). Finally, there is a *petite batterie*, (e.g., the fifth *enchaînement* in this lesson). As many steps as possible from the vocabulary for the year have been included in this lesson, but it would be clearly impossible to feature all the steps in a single lesson. Following is a brief discussion of the steps that were omitted from this class.

Emboîté en tournant.　Generally performed on a diagonal from the corner, it can include *petit saut de basque en tournant*: four *emboîtés* and two *sauts de basque*, linked by a step into the *saut de basque*. It can also be done from one side of the room to the other: six *emboîtés, tombé, coupé derrière, assemblé dessous*; repeat to the other side. In the sequence of the class it can either precede or follow the *grand allegro enchaînement*.

Ronds de jambe sautés.　Usually preceded by a *glissade* as preparation. It can be done with the *rond* at 45 degrees at a fairly fast speed or with a higher jump and a *double rond* at a slower speed. It could be included in the second *enchaînement* in this lesson: after closing in 5th position after the *cabriole*, *glissade sans changer* with the back leg, extend the back leg *à la seconde* as the push-off occurs; *double rond* in the air, the second *rond* ends as the landing occurs, close front; repeat *glissade rond sauté* to the other side. If these steps are added, the entire *enchaînement* is repeated to the same side and the same leg that started in front is in front at the end.

The *glissade ronds de jambe sautés* sequence is a good strength-building exercise for males and is valuable performed simply on its own.

Petits sautés in arabesque.　Usually linked with *petits sautés* in *seconde*. The body assumes the second *arabesque* position after a series of *sautés* in *seconde*, then the leg can be brought back to *seconde* for further *sautés*: from a *pirouette en dehors*, open leg *à la seconde*, continue turning with little hops on the supporting leg for a total of eight counts from the first *pirouette*; without stopping, shift the leg into *arabesque*, arms in oppositional *allongé*, continue hopping for another eight counts; shift the leg back *à la seconde*, continue the hops for twelve more counts; draw the leg into *retiré* with a *relevé* to *demi-pointe* on the supporting leg for the final *pirouettes*, end in 4th position *croisé*. These *pirouettes* are traditionally done toward the end of the lesson after the *grand allegro*.

Brisé volé.　Executed from the corner on a diagonal, these beats generally occur toward the end of the lesson. They can be performed on their own or in combination with regular *brisés*: four *brisés volés* and four *brisés en avant*.

Grands battements.

Révérence, or port de bras and révérence.

Pointe.　Now a separate lesson. It begins with exercises at the barre and includes all the vocabulary used up to this stage. A good source of material for center practice are recordings of classical variations from full-length ballets, such as *The Sleeping Beauty, Swan Lake*, and *Coppélia*.

At this level, exercises that promote strength should still be emphasized: *échappés* into 2nd and 4th positions; *relevés* on both legs and one leg, in *retiré* and big poses. Steps to be executed *en manège* include *piqués en dehors* and *en dedans* and *chaînés*.

For some students, the experience of *pointe* work may prove to be too painful. Some feet are not physically able to be used this way. It may be suggested to these students that they branch out into modern dance or jazz, where their classical training will serve as a good foundation.

VOCABULARY

The additions for this year consist of using the material learned previously in more challenging ways. At the barre, exercises can be combined more readily, and in the center, *enchaînements* with quick changes of weight and *pirouettes* condition the body to respond quickly and efficiently.

The men's class will emphasize strength and endurance as well as smooth transitions from one step to another.

Additional weekly classes are given in partnering and variations from the classical repertoire.

FOCUS AND EMPHASIS

During the first six years, the focus of instruction was on the acquisition of a pure, correct line and a clean execution of the classical vocabulary. With this foundation the individual quality of the dancer is free to emerge, but a distinction must still be made between the application of the technique to training and to choreography. The teacher, unlike the choreographer, is entrusted to impart the precepts of the art form. Although there is an element of choreography in all lessons, it is subordinate to the needs of the students. The lesson cannot be used as a choreographic platform.

In the last two years of study, kinetic awareness and intellectual understanding are sharpened. Although classical dancers are specialists, they need not be confined by the specifics of the technique. Awareness and understanding free them to explore and find expression in drastically different modes of movement. A major component in the process of reaching control of the craft is stylistic awareness—the ability to see the difference between a classical *balancé* and a modern triplet. The role of the teacher in these final, intensive years of study is to foster that awareness, to prevent mannerisms from creeping into the execution, and to guide students toward a full flowering of their talent.

To illustrate the Seventh Year, there are two sample lessons, which focus on different topics. The choice of topic for any particular class or series of classes is conditioned by those areas of the technique that need special attention. Classes should be devised to address these concerns systematically, and a class may be refocused, without compromising continuity, to answer an unexpected need.

The first lesson for the Seventh Year focuses on basic concepts: alignment, turn-out, balance. It also addresses classically correct configurations in the big poses on and off the floor, positions of the arms and head in relation to the legs, and accurate *épaulement* and appropriate transitions from one pose to another. This type of basic class is useful not only at this stage of training, but also during subsequent years as a means of reinforcing the fundamentals and the precepts of the technique.

The second lesson focuses on weight transference coupled with the application of *épaulement*. The use of *épaulement* in the classical technique is much more than an aesthetic consideration. It helps to organize the body mass around the center and to manipulate it with optimum efficiency. In order to push off the floor one must first apply pressure, then propel the body off. While this action is necessary in all jumps, in those from one foot it becomes a critical factor. The positioning of arms, shoulders, and head helps to maintain the weight over the supporting leg, ensuring not only a ballast for jumping off one leg, but also a safe landing because its impact is controlled by the body placed centrally over the supporting leg. This idea is best explained by this exercise: stand on one leg, the other leg in *demi-jambe* position, and hop on one leg; for the first few *temps levés* maintain the body's weight on the supporting side, then shift until the weight is equal on both sides of the body and try to jump again—the push-off is now very difficult, if not impossible. This simple experiment demonstrates how poorly many students attempt to jump.

Learning to jump actually begins with the first *plié* and the first *tendu*. The *plié* provides the means to push off the floor and the means to land safely. The *tendu* is the first experience of weight transference—standing on both feet in the closed position, transferring weight onto the supporting side as soon as the working leg begins to stretch outward, and replacing the weight onto both feet when the leg returns to the closed position. The final transfer of weight is often omitted; the student effectively stands on one leg throughout a series of *tendus*. This type of execution, while exercising the working leg, in no way addresses the full import of the intended action and does not prepare the body to respond quickly and efficiently.

It has become fashionable to execute *tendus* and *jetés* at the barre at breakneck speed. The adoption of this practice stems from a misunderstanding of the function of barre exercises, a blurring of boundaries between the movements done to condition the body and build the necessary musculature for the execution of the vocabulary and the actual application of those skills. The concept of weight transference is central to the process of acquiring a technique that serves, facilitates, and ensures safety in movement.

During the final two years of intensive study the kinetic experience of the classical technique can be complemented by an intellectual understanding of what makes movement happen. This understanding is the foundation for making subtle adjustments in execution of the vocabulary and honing the instrument to a truly expressive and responsive entity.

SAMPLE LESSON ONE

Barre
$\frac{6}{8}$ ♪ = 144

Pliés. One *grand plié*, one *relevé* to balance on *demi-pointe*, in 2nd, 1st, 4th, and 5th positions. Supporting arm lifts off the *barre* for each balance to the appropriate position.

Counts

1−4	*Grand plié* in 2nd position, arm from 2nd position through first *port de bras*.
5−7	Rise to *demi-pointe*, arm remains in 2nd position, other arm lifts off barre for balance.
8	Lower heels, *pointe tendue* with working leg, close to 1st position.
1−4	*Grand plié* in 1st position.
5−7	*Relevé* to *demi-pointe*, arms lower to *bras bas* for balance.
8	Lower heels, *dégagé* to *pointe tendue* to side, place working leg in 4th position *devant*.
1−4	*Grand plié* in 4th position.
5−7	Rise to *demi-pointe*, arms lower through *bras bas* to 3rd position *allongé devant*.
8	Lower heels, *pointe tendue devant*, close in 5th position.
1−4	*Grand plié* in 5th position.
5−8	Rise to *demi-pointe*, arms lower through *bras bas* to 5th position.

Note: A *port de bras cambré* can be added at the end of the sequence, either forward and back on flat foot and on *demi-pointe*, or *en rond*: bend forward, sideways toward barre, back; reverse going forward, sideways away from barre, back.

$\frac{4}{4}$ ♩ = 80

Battements tendus. Two *tendus* closing in 5th position, one *tendu* to open position, *demi-plié* on both feet, *pointe tendue*, close in 5th position; *en croix*.

Counts

1−2	From 5th position, *tendu devant*, arm in 2nd, close in 5th on second count.

Repeat once more.

1−2	Extend to *pointe tendue devant*, *demi-plié* on both legs in 4th position on count 2; arm sweeps to 1st position, head inclines toward barre.
3−4	*Pointe tendue*, arm returns to 2nd position; close in 5th position on count 4.

123

Repeat side, back, side.
Repeat entire combination once more.

$\frac{4}{4}$ ♩ = 92

Battements jetés. Two *jetés*, one *petit développé*; *en croix*. Repeat twice. Sixteen *balancés*, beginning front; hold last *balancé*, balance on *demi-pointe* in low *arabesque*. Arm in 2nd position throughout, in oppositional *allongé* for final balance.

Counts

And – 1   From 5th position, *jeté devant*.

Repeat once more.

And – 3   *Petit développé*: lift working foot to *demi-jambe* position, extend quickly to low *devant en l'air*.

And – 4   Close in 5th position.

Repeat to three remaining sides.

Repeat once more.

And – 1   Open to low *devant en l'air*.

And – 2   Passing through 1st position, extend to low *derrière*.

Repeat fourteen more times. Hold last position on *demi-pointe*, arm in oppositional *allongé devant*.

$\frac{6}{8}$ ♩. = 54

Ronds de jambe par terre. The preparation is part of the sequence, followed by six *ronds en dehors*, last one closes in 5th position back. Repeat sequence *en dedans*. Repeat once more *en dehors* and *en dedans*. A series of *cambrés*, working leg in *pointe tendue* front, side, and deep 4th position back.

Counts

1 – 3   From 5th position, *demi-plié* on supporting leg and extend working leg to *pointe tendue devant*, arm in 1st position, head tilted toward barre.

1 – 3   Open leg to 2nd position, straighten supporting leg, open arm to 2nd position.

1 – 3   *Rond en dehors*.

Repeat five more times. Close last one in 5th position back.

1 – 3   *Demi-plié* on supporting leg and extend working leg to *pointe tendue derrière*, arm in 1st position, head tilted toward barre.

1 – 3   Straighten supporting leg and open working leg to 2nd position. Open arm to 2nd position.

1 – 3   *Rond en dedans*.

Repeat five more times. Close last one in 5th position front.

Repeat *en dehors* and *en dedans* once more.

1—6   *Cambré* forward, *pointe tendue devant*.

1—6   *Cambré* back (see Fifth Year), close in 5th position, *pointe tendue* to side.

1—6   *Cambré* sideways toward barre, arm in 5th position.

1—6   Return to center, arm remains in 5th position, balance on *demi-pointe* in low *seconde* position, close in 5th position back.

1—6   Extend leg to *pointe tendue derrière*, supporting leg in *demi-plié*, *cambré* forward over front leg. Same as *pointe tendue derrière*.

1—6   Return to upright and straighten supporting leg, *cambré* back, arm in 5th position. Rise to *demi-pointe* for final balance, leg in *arabesque*, arms in 5th position.

$\frac{6}{8}$ ♩. = 54

Battements fondus.   *Double fondus en croix*; first *port de bras* with each *fondu*, second *port de bras* to 5th position with each *relevé*. Preparation: *pointe tendue à la seconde*.

Counts

1—6   *Fondu devant*.

1—6   Bring leg to *retiré* position and *demi-plié* on supporting leg, *relevé* to *demi-pointe*.

Repeat side, back, side.

Repeat adding a rise on *demi-pointe* to *fondu*. Hold and balance on last *retiré* position.

$\frac{2}{8}$ ♩ = 96

Battements frappés.   Four *frappés devant*, four *frappés à la seconde*, four *frappés derrière*, one *frappé à la seconde*, three *battements raccourcis*: accent toward the supporting leg with the foot fully pointed. Repeat beginning in back. Repeat sequence on *demi-pointe*. Balance in *attitude devant* for the final pose. Arm is in 2nd position throughout. Preparation: *pointe tendue à la seconde*.

Counts

And—1   *Frappé devant*.

Repeat three more times.

Repeat side and back.

And—1   *Frappé* to side, open leg a little higher.

And – 2   *Raccourci*: bring leg to *demi-jambe* with strong accent toward supporting leg.

Repeat twice more, opening on "and."

Repeat, beginning to back.

Repeat sequence on *demi-pointe*. Raise leg to *attitude devant* for balance.

$\frac{3}{4}$ ♩ = 120

Ronds de jambe en l'air.   Two *retirés passés*, two *ronds en dehors*. Repeat with *ronds en dedans*. Repeat with a rise to *demi-pointe* for each *retiré* and for the *ronds*. Balance in *attitude* at the end of the sequence.

Counts

1 – 3	From 5th position, working leg in front, arm in 2nd position, *retiré passé* close in 5th position back, arm extends to *allongé seconde*, head turns toward arm.
1 – 3	*Retiré passé* close in 5th position front, arm returns to 2nd position, head returns to face front as leg closes.
1	Open leg *à la seconde* to 90 degrees.
2 – 3	*Rond en dehors*.
1 – 2	*Rond en dehors*.
3	Close in 5th position back.

Repeat sequence, close *retirés* front and back, *ronds en dedans*.

Repeat entire sequence with rise to *demi-pointe* when leg is lifted and lower to flat foot in 5th position. End with *passé* to *attitude* and balance.

$\frac{2}{4}$ ♩ = 69

Adagio.   *Développé devant*, *passé* and *développé à la seconde*, *demi-grand rond de jambe* to *devant*, *grand rond de jambe en dehors*, end in *arabesque*. Reverse sequence with *développé derrière*, *à la seconde*, *demi-grand rond* to *derrière*, *grand rond en dedans*, end in *devant en l'air*. Repeat on *demi-pointe*.

Counts

1 – 4	From 5th position, *développé devant*, arm rises to 5th position.
1 – 4	*Passé* to *développé à la seconde*, arm lowers to 2nd position.
1 – 4	*Demi-grand rond* to *devant*, arm remains in 2nd position.
1 – 4	*Grand rond de jambe* to *derrière*, arm shifts to *allongé devant* as leg arrives in back. Close in

5th position back. Repeat, beginning with *développé* back, arm lifts to 5th position when leg comes to *devant* position.

Repeat on *demi-pointe*. Hold last position, arms in 5th position for balance.

$\frac{2}{4}$ ♩ = 112

Petits battements sur le cou-de-pied. Four slow *battements* beating evenly back and front, four with front position accented, eight faster *battements* on *demi-pointe*. Repeat four times. Arm remains in *bras bas*. End with *jambe dans-la-main*. Preparation: *pointe tendue à la seconde*.

Counts

1–4   Place working foot on *cou-de-pied devant* and beat evenly back and front.

And–1 Beat back and stop front.

Repeat three more times.

1–8   Rise to *demi-pointe*, beat evenly back and front.

Repeat sequence three more times. Lift working leg to *retiré* and *demi-plié* on supporting leg, take heel in hand, extend leg front, open to side and straighten supporting leg; release heel, leg remains in high extension; balance, arms in 5th position.

$\frac{6}{8}$ ♩. = 92
March

Grands battements. With back to *barre*, arm stretched along support: seven *grands battements* to front, *dégagé à la seconde* to change feet. Repeat with other leg. Turn sideways to *barre*: seven *grands battements à la seconde*. Turn to other side and repeat. Turn to face *barre*, both hands on the support: seven *grands battements* to back, *dégagé* to change feet. Repeat with other leg.

Counts

And–1 *Grand battement*, close in 5th position.

Repeat six more times.

And–1 *Pointe tendue à la seconde* with working leg, close in 5th position back.

Repeat with other leg. Turn to first side on count 8.

Repeat with seven *battements à la seconde*. Turn to other side on count 8.

Repeat on other side. Turn toward *barre* on count 8.

Repeat with seven *battements* to back. Change feet: *tendu à la seconde* with working leg, close in 5th position front.

Repeat to back with second leg.

127

Center

$\frac{2}{4}$ $\downarrow$ = 126

Stretching. Leg on barre, *cambré*, slide to split, or students can do their own stretching at barre or in center.

Port de bras. *Temps liés* with *pirouettes* (see Fifth Year). Instead of *pointe tendue* position, working leg is raised to 90 degrees. Timing and arm positions remain the same as in the cited description.

Battements tendus with pirouettes. Four *battements tendus dessus*, *retiré* on *demi-pointe* (preparation), *pirouettes en dehors*; four *tendus croisé devant*, four *tendus croisé derrière* with other leg. Repeat on other side. Repeat with *tendus dessous*, *pirouettes en dedans*, *tendus derrière* and *devant*.

Counts

And – 1 From 5th position, arms in 2nd position, *tendu* with back leg, close in 5th position front.

Repeat with other leg.

Repeat two more times.

And – 1 *Retiré* and *relevé* on *demi-pointe*, front leg raised, same arm as working leg in 1st position.

And – 2 *Demi-plié* on both legs in 5th position, working leg in front.

And – 4 *Pirouettes en dehors*, close in 5th position back.

And – 1 *Tendu croisé devant*, arms in 4th position oppositional.

Repeat three more times.

And – 1 *Tendu croisé derrière*, arms in 4th position complementary.

Repeat three more times.

Repeat on other side.

Repeat with *tendus dessous* and *pirouettes en dedans*. *Retiré* with back leg, *demi-plié* with working leg in back, arms in complementary 4th position, *pirouettes* end in front.

$\frac{3}{4}$ $\downarrow$ = 100
Mazurka

Pas de basque, battements frappés, and ronds de jambe en l'air. Two *pas de basque en avant*, *coupé* to bring front foot on *cou-de-pied*, six *battements frappés* in *écarté* direction, three *ronds de jambe en l'air* (*en dehors*, *en dedans*, *en dehors*), close in 5th position between each *rond*; *sous-sus*.

Counts

And – 3 From 5th position, *pas de basque en avant*, close in 5th position back.

And – 3 *Pas de basque en avant* with other leg, end with *coupé* under and bring front leg to *cou-de-pied*;

arms through first *port de bras* with each *pas de basque*.

1 – 6   *Battement frappé* in *seconde écarté*, arm in complementary 4th position *devant*; last *frappé* lifts leg to 90 degrees, arms open to 2nd position, body turns to *en face*.

1 – 3   *Rond en l'air en dehors*, close in 5th position back on count 3.

And – 3   Open leg to 90 degrees, *rond en dedans*, close in 5th position front on count 3.

And – 3   *Rond en dehors*, close in 5th position back.

1 – 3   *Demi-plié, sous-sus*, arms rise to 5th position.

Repeat on other side.

$\frac{4}{4}$ ♩ - 60

Adagio.   *Grand plié* in 4th position with *port de bras* to 1st position, *relevé* to *demi-pointe*, arms in 3rd position *allongé*; *dégagé* to *pointe tendue*, close in 5th position front; *développé croisé devant, demi-grand rond de jambe* to *écarté devant*; *fouetté* into first *arabesque; promenade en dedans*, end in *attitude croisée*, balance on *demi-pointe*; stretch working leg and extend into deep lunge in 4th position *(demi-plié* on front leg, back leg straight), *grand port de bras en rond*, straighten front leg, back leg in *pointe tendue*, lower heel (preparation), *pirouettes en dehors*, end in 4th position, arms in *seconde allongé* back arched.

Counts

1 – 4   In 4th position *croisé, grand plié*, arms lower from 2nd position through *bras bas* to 1st position.

5 – 8   Rise on *demi-pointe*, arms extend to *allongé* in 3rd position.

1 – 4   Lower heels into a *demi-plié* and extend front leg to *pointe tendue devant*, close in 5th position front, arms through 2nd positon to *bras bas*.

5 – 8   *Développé croisé devant*, arms in oppositional 4th position.

1 – 4   *Demi-grand rond de jambe* to *écarté devant*, arms to complementary 4th position: 5th position arm lowers to 2nd position, other arm rises to 5th position through 1st position.

5 – 8   Turn body toward side of room, leaving uplifted leg behind: *fouetté* to first *arabesque*, arms shift to first *arabesque* position.

1 – 8   *Promenade en dedans*, toward supporting leg.

129

1–4	*Attitude croisé*, arms in oppositional 4th position.
5–8	Rise and balance on *demi-pointe*.
1–4	Extend working leg, *demi-plié* on supporting leg and lower working leg into wide 4th position, arms remain in oppositional 4th position.
5–8	*Grand port de bras*: bend forward over front leg, sideways toward back leg, uplifted arm opens to 2nd position, other arm rises to 5th position.
1–4	Complete circular movement by bending back, return body to upright, arms return to oppositional 4th position.
5–8	Straighten supporting leg, back leg in *pointe tendue derrière*, arms remain.
1–4	Lower back heel, lower uplifted arm to 1st position, *demi-plié* on front leg (preparation).
5–8	*Pirouettes en dehors*, end in deep 4th position, working leg in back, arm extended slightly behind the shoulders in 2nd position *allongé*, head turned toward front arm, upper back arched.
1–4	Hold.

Repeat on other side.

$\frac{2}{4}$ ♩ = 92

Allegro. Two *changements*, one *échappé* to 4th position, one *échappé* to 2nd position, one *échappé* to 4th position.

Counts

And–1	From 5th position, *changement*, arms in *bras bas*.
And–2	*Changement.*
And–3	*Echappé* to 4th position, arms in oppositional 4th position *devant*.
And–4	Jump back to 5th position, arms open to 2nd position.
And–1	*Echappé* into 2nd position, arms in 2nd position.
And–2	Jump back to 5th position, original front foot in back.
And–3	*Echappé* to 4th position, arms in oppositional 4th position *devant*.
And–4	Jump back to 5th position, arms lower to *bras bas*.

Repeat on other side.

$\frac{4}{4}$ ♩ = 92

Allegro. *Glissade sans changer, assemblé dessus, petit jeté dessus, temps levé, three pas de chat, pas de bourrée dessous.*

Counts

And – 1 From 5th position, back leg initiates *glissade*, arms lower from 2nd position to *bras bas*.

And – 2 *Assemblé dessus*, close back leg 5th position front, arms rise through first *port de bras*.

And – 3 *Jeté dessus*, back leg intitiates jump, arms in complementary 4th position *devant*.

And – 4 *Temps levé*, arms remain.

And – 1 *Pas de chat*, arms to oppositional 4th position *devant*.

Repeat *pas de chat* twice more.

And – 4 *Pas de bourrée dessous*, arms open to 2nd position.

Repeat *pas de chat* on other side.

$\frac{3}{4}$ ♩ = 176

Allegro. Three *sissonnes croisé en avant*, one *sissonne changé croisé*, four *sissonnes de côté dessus*. This *enchaînement* can be reversed: *sissonnes en arrière, sissonnes dessous*.

Counts

1 – 3 *Sissonne en avant*: from 5th position open back leg in low *derrière* position, arms in oppositional 4th position *allongé devant*.

Repeat twice more, arms remain.

1 – 3 *Sissonne changé*: after push-off, front leg slips back to low *arabesque*, arms to oppositional 4th position on other side.

1 – 3 *Sissonne de côté dessus*: open back leg to low *seconde*, close in front, arms in 2nd position for jump and complementary 4th position *devant* as landing occurs.

Repeat three more times.

Repeat to other side.

$\frac{3}{4}$ ♩ = 108

Allegro. Two *tombé coupé temps de ciseaux*; two *tombé coupé grand jeté* into second *arabesque ouverte*.

Note: This *enchaînement* is performed to a mazurka.

Counts

1 From 5th position, *tombé* onto front leg, arms in complementary 4th position *devant*, body leaning over front leg.

2	*Coupé*: back leg cuts, releasing front leg into *battement*.
3	*Temps de ciseaux*: front leg kicks in front as jump begins, other leg kicks in front, arms rise to 5th position, body turns from *croisé* to *croisé* on other side, as landing occurs upper body arches and arms open out.

Repeat on other side.

1	*Tombé*.
2	*Coupé*.
3	*Jeté*: front leg kicks in *effacé* direction, arms in second *arabesque* position.

Repeat on other side.

Repeat entire sequence.

$\frac{3}{4}$ ♩ = 176
Waltz

Allegro. *Pas de bourrée couru, grand jeté* into *attitude*, on a diagonal from the corner. Preparation: *dégagé pointe tendue croisé devant*.

Counts

And – 3 *Pas de bourrée couru*, arms lower to *bras bas* during run.

And – 3 *Croisé* leg kicks in front, other leg lifts back in *attitude*, arms rise to oppositional 4th position.

Repeat.

$\frac{2}{4}$ ♩ = 168

Allegro. Three *entrechat-quatre*, one *royal* or *entrechat-six*.

Counts

And – 1 From 5th position, *entrechat-quatre*, arms in *bras bas*, body in *croisé épaulé* position.

Repeat twice more.

And – 4 *Royal* or *entrechat-six*; arms may open to 2nd position on the *entrechat-six*; body shifts to *croisé épaulé* on other side.

Repeat on other side.

Grands battements. Eight *grands battements en montant* (*dessous*), eight *grands battements en descendant* (*dessus*), arms in 2nd position.

Révérence.

SAMPLE LESSON TWO

Barre
$\frac{4}{4}$ ♩ = 48

Pliés. One *grand plié*, one rise through the feet to *demi-pointe* and roll down through the feet to replace the heels on the floor, one *cambré*. In 2nd, 1st, 4th, and 5th positions.

Counts

1–4   *Grand plié* in 2nd, arm in first *port de bras*.

1–4   *Demi-plié*, lift heels off floor, pushing up through feet and straighten knees, hold on *demi-pointe*.

1–4   Remain on *demi-pointe*, and bend knees, roll down through feet, straighten knees after heels touch floor.

1–4   *Cambré* forward; *pointe tendue* and close in 1st position.

Repeat *grand plié* and rise through feet; *cambré* sideways toward barre, *pointe tendue* to side, place working foot in 4th position front.

Repeat *plié* and rise; *cambré* back, *pointe tendue devant*, close in 5th position.

Repeat *plié* and rise; *port de bras en rond: cambré* forward, toward barre, back, and upright. Balance in 5th position, arms in 5th position.

$\frac{4}{4}$ ♩ = 176

Battements tendus. One *tendu devant, dégagé* to *pointe tendue devant, demi-plié* in 4th position, *pointe tendue derrière* with other leg, close in 5th position; one *tendu à la seconde* with original working leg, close in 5th position back; one *tendu derrière, degagé* to *pointe tendue derrière, demi-plié* in 4th position, *pointe tendue devant* with other leg, close in 5th position front; one *tendu à la seconde* with working leg, close in 5th position front; two *tendus à la seconde, pointe tendue à la seconde, demi-plié* in 2nd position, *pointe tendue* with other leg, *demi-plié* in 2nd position, *pointe tendue* with original working leg; three *tendus*, close in 1st position, one *tendu*, close in 5th position back. Repeat, beginning with *tendu derrière*.

Counts

1–2   From 5th position, *tendu devant*, arm in 2nd position.

3   *Pointe tendue devant*, arm lowers to *bras bas*.

4   *Demi-plié* in 4th position.

5   Extend back leg to *pointe tendue derrière*, arm in *allongé devant*.

133

6	Close in 5th position back.
7 – 8	*Tendu à la seconde* with original working leg, close in 5th position back.

Repeat sequence, in reverse, beginning with *tendu derrière*, arm rises to 5th position when second leg is *devant*.

1 – 2	*Tendu à la seconde*, close in 5th position back.
3 – 4	*Tendu à la seconde*, close in 5th position front.
5	*Degagé* to *pointe tendue seconde*.
6	*Demi-plié* in 2nd position.
7 – 8	*Pointe tendue seconde* with other leg, body in *écarté devant*, working arm in 2nd position *allongée*, other arm uplifted, head turned toward barre.
1	*Demi-plié* in 2nd position.
2	*Pointe tendue seconde* with original working leg, arms and body in *écarté devant* position.
3 – 4	Hold *écarté* position.
5	Close in 1st position.
6	*Tendu à la seconde*, close in 1st position.
7	*Tendu*, close in 1st position.
8	*Tendu*, close in 5th position back, arm in 2nd position for last four *tendus*.

Repeat sequence, beginning in back.

$\frac{2}{4}$ ♩ = 192

Battements jetés. Four *jetés devant*; four *jetés derrière* with other leg; four *jetés à la seconde* closing in 5th position, four *jetés à laseconde* closing in 1st position (the last *jeté* closes in 5th position back to reverse the exercise).

Counts

And – 1 From 5th position *jeté devant*, arm in 5th position.

Repeat three more times.

And – 1 *Jeté derrière* with other leg, arm in *allongé devant*.

Repeat three more times.

And – 1 *Jeté à la seconde* with first leg, arm in 2nd position, close in 5th position back.

Repeat three more times, close alternately front and back.

And – 1 *Jeté à la seconde*, close in 1st position, arm lowers to *bras bas*. Repeat three more times, close last one in 5th position.

Repeat in reverse.

$\frac{3}{4}$ $\quad \bullet = 152$

Ronds de jambe par terre. Four *ronds en dehors*, *demi-plié* in 1st position, *relevé* on supporting leg, working leg in low *effacé devant en l'air* position, *tombé* onto working leg and *piqué* back onto supporting leg, lower working leg through *demi-plié* in 1st position and extend in *pointe tendue derrière*, two *ronds jetés en dehors*, end with *dégagé* to *pointe tendue devant*. Repeat sequence *en dedans*. End with *grand port de bras* in deep 4th position. Preparation: (see Fourth Year). Repeat three more times.

Counts

1–3   *Rond en dehors*, arm in 2nd position.

Repeat three more times

1–3   *Demi-plié* in 1st position and *relevé*, working leg lifted to *effacé devant*, arm in 2nd position, head turned toward barre.

1–3   *Tombé* onto working leg into *demi-plié*, other leg extended *effacé derrière*, supporting arm lifted in 2nd position *allongée*.

1–3   *Piqué* back onto supporting leg on *demi-pointe*, working leg again in *effacé devant*.

1–3   Lower working leg, *demi-plié* in 1st position, extend working leg to *pointe tendue derrière*, arm in 2nd position.

1–6   Pass working leg through 1st position to *devant en l'air*, *rond en dehors en l'air*.

Repeat once more. Pass working leg through 1st position to *pointe tendue devant*.

Repeat entire sequence *en dedans*.

End with *grand port de bras* in deep 4th position, weight on original supporting leg (see Sixth Year).

$\frac{3}{4}$ $\quad \bullet = 144$

Battements fondus. Two *fondus devant*, one *fondu à la seconde*, *tombé piqué*. Reverse, beginning with *fondus* back. Preparation: *pointe tendue à la seconde*.

Counts

1–6   *Fondu devant*, arm through first *port de bras*.

1–6   *Fondu devant*.

1–6   *Fondu à la seconde*.

1–3   *Tombé* onto working leg, other leg in *seconde en l'air*, hold *demi-plié*, arms in 2nd position.

4–6   *Piqué* onto original supporting leg, working leg extended in *seconde en l'air*.

Repeat, beginning with *fondu derrière*.

135

Repeat entire sequence, rising on *demi-pointe* with each *fondu* and *piqué* onto *demi-pointe*.

$\frac{4}{4}$ ♩ = 132

Battements frappés. Four *frappés devant*, four *frappés à la seconde*, two *frappés double à la seconde*; *demi-plié* and *relevé* with half turn *en dehors*, *demi-plié relevé* with half turn *en dedans* to original side, working leg in *retiré* position for turns. Repeat in reverse, beginning with *frappés* back, *relevé en dedans* and *en dehors*. Preparation: *pointe tendue à la seconde*.

Counts

1   *Frappé devant*, arm in 2nd position.
Repeat three more times.

1   *Frappé à la seconde*.
Repeat three more times.

1 – 2   *Frappé double*: beat front, back, *à la seconde*.
3 – 4   *Frappé double*: beat back, front, *à la seconde*.
5 – 6   *Demi-plié* on supporting leg, working leg remains extended, *relevé* and bring working leg to *retiré* with half turn *en dehors*.
7 – 8   *Demi-plié* and *relevé* with half turn to face original side.
Repeat, beginning with *frappés derrière*.
Repeat entire sequence on *demi-pointe*.

$\frac{3}{4}$ ♩ = 152

Ronds de jambe en l'air. *Demi-plié* on supporting leg and lift working leg to *attitude devant*; *demi-grand rond de jambe à la seconde*, supporting leg straightens; four *ronds en dehors*; lower leg to *pointe tendue*, close in 5th position back. Repeat, beginning with *attitude derrière* and *ronds en dedans*, close in 5th position front. All the *ronds en l'air* can be doubles. Repeat entire sequence on *demi-pointe*. End with *fouetté en dehors*, ending in *attitude*.

Counts

1 – 3   From 5th position, lift working leg to *attitude devant*, supporting leg in *demi-plié*, arm in 1st position.
4 – 6   Carry leg *à la seconde* and straighten both knees, arm opens to 2nd position.
1 – 3   *Rond en dehors*.
Repeat three more times.

1 – 3   Lower leg to *pointe tendue*.
4 – 6   Close in 5th position back.
Repeat sequence, beginning back.
Repeat on *demi-pointe*.

$\frac{4}{4}$ ♩ = 60

Adagio. *Développé croisé devant; passé, développé à la seconde; tombé* onto original working leg, other leg in *pointe tendue* to side; *cambrè* sideways toward supporting leg; *piqué* onto original supporting leg, other leg in *arabesque* facing *barre*; close in 5th position with quarter turn. Repeat on other side.

Note: This exercise can be repeated on *demi-pointe* or performed in reverse, beginning with *développé croisé derrière,* and ending with *piqué* into an extension *devant en l'air* with back to barre.

Counts

1 – 4	*Développé croisé devant*, arm in 2nd position, head turned away from barre.
1 – 4	*Passé, développé à la seconde,* arm through first *port de bras*.
1 – 4	Rise to *demi-pointe, tombé* onto working leg into *demi-plié,* other leg extended in *pointe tendue seconde, cambré de côté* away from extended leg, original working arm in *bras bas,* other arm in 5th position.
1 – 4	Return to upright, *piqué* into *arabesque* facing barre, both hands on support, close in 5th position.

Repeat on other side.

Repeat in reverse: with *développé croisé derrière,* head is turned toward barre, *tombé cambré* sequence is the same, shift body back to barre with *piqué,* working leg extended *en l'air devant,* both hands on support.

$\frac{4}{4}$ ♩ = 132

Petits battements sur le cou-de-pied. Six *petits battements, tombé* into 5th position, *coupé* with original supporting leg and open working leg to low *en l'air seconde;* arm in *bras bas* for *petits battements,* opens to 2nd position for *tombé coupé dégagé.* Repeat, alternating *tombé coupé* front and back (*dessus* and *dessous*). Preparation: *pointe tendue à la seconde.*

Counts

1 – 5	*Petits battements,* beating alternately back and front.
6	Open working leg to low *seconde*.
7	*Tombé dessus:* bring working leg to 5th position *devant* and *demi-plié,* other leg in *retiré à demi-jambe derrière.*
8	Place back leg on floor (*coupé*) and open working leg to low *en l'air seconde.*

137

Repeat *petits battements, coupé dessous*, other leg raised in *demi-jambe devant*.
Repeat on *demi-pointe*.

$\frac{4}{4}$ ♩ = 112
March

Grands battements. One *grand battement devant*, one *grand battement derrière* with other leg, two *grands battements à la seconde* with original working leg; arm in 2nd position throughout. Repeat, beginning with *battement* back. Repeat entire sequence once more.

Counts

And – 1 From 5th position, *battement devant*.

And – 2 *Grand battement derrière* with other leg.

And – 1 *Battement à la seconde* with original working leg, close in 5th position front.

And – 2 *Battement à la seconde*, close in 5th position back.

Repeat sequence, *battement derrière, devant, à la seconde*.

Center
$\frac{3}{4}$ ♩ = 120

Port de bras. From 5th position, *chassé en avant* to *pointe tendue effacé derrière*, *demi-plié* in 4th position and transfer weight onto back leg (*lié*), front leg in *pointe tendue effacé devant*; *balancé* through 1st position to second *arabesque croisée*, rise on *demi-pointe* to balance; *demi-plié* on supporting leg, *relevé*, bring working leg to *retiré* position and turn *en dehors*; *tombé* onto working leg, *pas de bourrée dessous*, close in 5th position; *dégagé* to *pointe tendue devant*, preparation in 4th position, *pirouettes en dehors*. Repeat to other side.

Counts

1 – 3 From 5th position, *chassé en avant* in *effacé* direction, arms open to oppositional 4th position through *bras bas* and 1st position.

1 – 3 Hold *pointe tendue effacé derrière*.

1 – 3 *Demi-plié* on both legs in 4th position, transfer weight onto back leg, front leg extended in *pointe tendue effacé*.

1 – 3 Hold, arms remain in oppositional 4th position.

1 – 3 *Balancé* through 1st position to *arabesque croisé*, arms meet in 1st position, extend to oppositional *allongé* (second *arabesque* position).

1 – 3 Slowly rise on *demi-pointe*.

1 – 3 Balance on *demi-pointe*.

1 – 3 *Demi-plié* on supporting leg.

1 – 3	*Relevé*, bring working leg to *retiré*, and turn *en dehors* (a very controlled slow *pirouette)*.
1 – 3	*Tombé* onto working leg front, other leg in *demi-jambe derrière*, arms in complementary 4th position *devant*.
1 – 3	*Pas de bourrée dessous*, end in 5th position, arms open to 2nd position.
1 – 3	*Dégagé* to *pointe tendue croisé devant*, arms in oppositional 4th position *devant*.
1 – 3	Lower front heel and *demi-plié* (preparation).
1 – 3	*Pirouettes en dehors*, end in 4th position, working leg in back.
1 – 3	Hold.
1 – 3	Back leg to *pointe tendue*, close in 5th position.

Repeat sequence on other side.

$\frac{4}{4}$ ♩ = 84

Battements tendus and jetés. *Dégagé croisé devant* to *pointe tendue*, *lié* to *pointe tendue croisé derrière*, close in 5th position. Reverse. *Dégagé* to *pointe tendue seconde*, *lié* and extend other foot to *pointe tendue*, close in 5th position front; one *tendu* with back leg to side, close front; two *jetés* to side, close back then front; *dégagé* to low *en l'air croisé devant* and *relevé* on supporting leg, *lié* through 4th position and *relevé* on front leg, back leg in low *arabesque croisée*, close in 5th position. Reverse. *Dégagé* to side in low *en l'air* and *relevé* on supporting leg; *lié* through 2nd position to *relevé* on original working leg, other leg in low extension to side, close in 5th position front; *retiré passé* with front leg to 4th position *derrière* (preparation), *fouettés en dedans*, end in 5th position front. Repeat to other side.

Counts

1	From 5th position, open leg to *pointe tendue croisé devant*, arms in oppositional 4th position.
2	*Demi-plié* on both legs in 4th position (*lié*).
3	*Pointe tendue derrière* with back leg, arms remain.
4	Close in 5th position, arms lower to *bras bas*.
1	Open back leg to *pointe tendue croisé derrière*, arms in oppositional 4th position.
2	*Demi-plié* in 4th position.
3	*Pointe tendue croisé devant* with front leg.
4	Close in 5th position, arms to *bras bas*.
1	*Dégagé* to *pointe tendue seconde* with front leg, arms open to 2nd position.

2	*Lié* through 2nd position.
3	*Pointe tendue* with other leg.
4	Close in 5th position front.
1–2	*Tendu à la seconde* with back leg, close in 5th position front.
3	*Battement jeté à la seconde* with same leg, close in 5th position back.
4	*Jeté à la seconde*, close in 5th position front.
1	*Relevé* on back leg and extend front leg to low *en l'air croisé devant*, arms in oppositional 4th position.
2	*Lié* through 4th position.
3	*Relevé* on front leg, back leg extended in low *arabesque croisée*.
4	Close in 5th position back, arms return to *bras bas*.
1	*Relevé* on front leg, back leg in low *arabesque croisée*, arms in oppositional 4th position.
2	*Lié* through 4th position.
3	*Relevé* on back leg, front leg in low *croisé devant*.
4	Close in 5th position front, arms return to *bras bas*.
1	*Relevé* on back leg, front leg extended in low *seconde*, arms in 2nd position.
2	*Lié* through 2nd position.
3	*Relevé* on working leg, other leg in low *seconde*.
4	Close in 5th position front.
1–2	*Relevé* to *retiré* position with front leg, place in 4th position *croisé*, arms in complementary 4th position *devant*.
3–4	*Fouettés en dedans*, arms in 1st position, close in 5th position front.

Repeat sequence on other side.

$\frac{3}{4}$ ♩ = 120

Ronds de jambe en l'air.   One *rond de jambe en dehors*, *passé* through *retiré* and *développé effacé devant*, supporting leg in *demi-plié*; straighten supporting leg and return working leg *à la seconde, rond en dedans, passé* to *développé effacé derrière*, supporting leg in *demi-plié*; *balancé* through 1st position to *en l'air croisé devant* and *relevé* to *demi-pointe; tombé* into wide 4th position, front leg in *demi-plié*, pirouettes in *attitude en dehors*, end in *croisé*; extend leg to *arabesque croisée* and rise on *demi-pointe; pas de bourrée en tournant en dehors*. Repeat to other side.

Counts

1 – 3	From 5th position open front leg *à la seconde en l'air.*
4 – 6	*Rond en dehors*, arms in 2nd position.
7 – 9	*Passé* to *développé effacé devant*, supporting leg in *demi-plié*, arms in oppositional 4th position *devant.*
1 – 3	Return *à la seconde*, body *en face*, arms in 2nd position.
4 – 6	*Rond en dedans.*
7 – 9	*Passé* to *développé effacé derrière*, arms in 2nd position *allongé*, front arm higher, supporting leg in *demi-plié.*
1 – 3	*Balancé* through 1st position to *en l'air croisé devant* and *relevé* on supporting leg, arms in oppositional 4th position.
4 – 6	*Tombé* to 4th position, front leg in *demi-plié*, arms in oppositional 4th position *devant* (preparation).
7 – 9	*Pirouettes en dehors* in *attitude.*
1 – 3	End *pirouettes* in *croisé*, remain in *attitude.*
4 – 6	Stretch working leg into *arabesque* and *relevé* on supporting leg.
7 – 9	*Pas de bourrée en tournant:* remain in *relevé*, bring working leg down for *pas de bourrée*, turning toward back foot, end in 5th position.

Repeat sequence on other side.

$\frac{4}{4}$ ♩ = 60

Adagio.   From *pointe tendue croisée derrière*, pass back leg through high *retiré* to *développé effacé devant*, supporting leg in *demi-plié*, *piqué* onto working leg, other leg in first *arabesque*. Repeat *passé* and *développé piqué* into *arabesque* on other side. *Demi-plié* on supporting leg, step back onto back leg (*lié*) and raise front leg in *effacé devant*, balancé through 1st position to second *arabesque croisée*, *promenade en dehors* and gradually bring uplifted leg from *arabesque* to *devant*, end in *croisé (fouetté)*; rise to *demi-pointe* and *tombé* into wide 4th position, *grand port de bras en rond*; return center to *pointe tendue derrière*, lower back heel (preparation); *pirouettes à la seconde en dedans*; end with *fouetté* into first *arabesque*; end with *chassé* through 1st position to *pointe tendue derrière.* Repeat on other side.

Counts

1 – 4	*Passé* through *retiré* and *développé effacé devant*, arms in oppositional 4th position.

5—8	*Demi-plié* on supporting leg, *piqué* into first *arabesque*.
1—4	*Passé* and *développé* into *effacé devant*, arms in oppositional 4th position.
5—8	*Demi-plié*, *piqué* into first *arabesque*.
1—4	*Demi-plié*, step back onto working leg, other leg lifted to *effacé devant*, arms in oppositional 4th position.
5—8	*Balancé* through 1st position to second *arabesque croisée*.
1—8	*Promenade en dehors* (toward the uplifted leg): when body faces first upstage corner, begin to rotate toward leg, leaving it in same place (*fouetté*), end in *croisé devant*, arms in oppositional 4th position.
1—4	Rise on *demi-pointe*, *tombé* onto front leg, arms remain in 4th position.
1—8	*Grand port de bras en rond*.
1—4	Return center to *pointe tendue croisé derrière*, arms in oppositional 4th position, lower heel, arms in complementary 4th position *devant*.
5—8	*Pirouettes en dedans à la seconde*, arms in 5th position, end in first *arabesque*, arms to first *arabesque* position.
1—4	*Chassé* through 1st position, step onto front leg, other leg in *pointe tendue derrière*, arms in 5th position.

Repeat sequence on other side.

$\frac{2}{4}$ ♩ = 96

Allegro. *Echappé* into 4th position *croisé*; *échappé* into 2nd position, *pas de bourrée dessous*; two *petits jetés dessus*; *soutenu en tournant en dedans*. Repeat to other side.

Note: This *enchaînement* can be reversed: the *échappés* are the same, followed by *pas de bourrée dessus*, two *petits jetés dessous*, and *soutenu en dehors*.

Counts

And—1	From 5th position, *échappé* into 4th position *croisé*, arms in oppositional 4th position *devant*.
And—2	Jump, close in 5th position.
And—3	*Echappé* to 2nd position, arms in 2nd position.
And—4	*Pas de bourrée dessous*: transfer weight onto original front foot, initiate *bourrée* with other leg, close in 5th position, second leg front.

And – 1   *Petit jeté dessus:* open back leg to low *seconde*, jump onto it, other leg to *demi-jambe* in back, arms in complementary 4th position *devant*.

And – 2   *Petit jeté* with second leg; back leg passes through 5th position before opening to side for jump, arms in complementary 4th position *devant*.

And – 3   *Soutenu en dedans:* open *demi-jambe* leg to low *en l'air seconde*, arms in 2nd position.

And – 4   Bring working leg to 5th position front and rise on *demi-pointe*, arms in *bras bas*; swivel toward back leg, which comes to front, arms rise to 5th position; end on *demi-pointe*.

Repeat sequence on other side, beginning with quick *demi-plié.*

$\frac{3}{4}$ ♩ = 104

Allegro.   Two *ballonnés composés en avant*, one *pas de basque en avant*, one *ballonné composé en arrière*. This *enchaînement* can be reversed: two *ballonnés composés en arrière*, one *pas de basque en arrière*, one *ballonné composé en avant*. It is performed to a mazurka.

Counts

1   From 5th position, *ballonné devant*, with front leg.

2 – 3   From *demi-jambe* position, slide working foot through 5th position to 4th position, straighten legs to *pointe tendue derrière*, arms in oppositional 4th position.

Repeat, arms remain.

1 – 3   *Pas de basque en avant*: open front leg to *pointe tendue devant, demi-rond par terre à la seconde,* step onto working leg, pass other leg through 1st position, step forward onto it, original leg in *pointe tendue derrière,* close in 5th position, arms open through *bras bas* to front.

1 – 3   *Ballonné composé*: extend back leg for *ballonné,* step back and extend front leg to *pointe tendue croisée devant,* arms in oppositional 4th position.

Repeat sequence to other side.

$\frac{3}{4}$ ♩ = 112

Allegro.   *Sissonne ouverte de côté, coupé dessous, assemblé dessous*. Repeat three times. *Echappé* into 4th position *effacé, temps levé* into *arabesque, pas de bourrée dessous*. For men, the last three steps can be replaced by *sous-sus* and *tours en l'air*. Repeat on other side.

Counts

1	From 5th position, open front leg through *déve-loppé* to high *seconde*, arms open to complementary 4th position (same arm up as lifted leg) through *bras bas*, body leans away from extended leg.
2	Step behind supporting leg for *coupé*, arms in 2nd position.
3	*Assemblé*, close in 5th position back.

Repeat twice more.

1	*Echappé* into 4th position *effacé*, arms in oppositional 4th position *devant*.
2	Spring up onto front leg, other leg extended in *arabesque*, arms in second *arabesque* position.
3	*Pas de bourrée dessous*, arms return to *bras bas*.

Repeat sequence on other side.

$\frac{3}{4}$ ♩ = 208

Allegro.   From upstage center, three *failli fouetté sauté; failli*, two steps, *grand jeté; pas de bourrée couru* and *grand jeté*; two steps, *piqué* to second *arabesque croisée*; two *pas de bourrée couru, grand jeté en tournant*.

Note: This *enchaînement* travels from side to side.

Counts

1−3	From 5th position, *failli*, back leg to 4th position *croisé* in front, arms in 1st position.
4−6	*Fouetté sauté*: kick back leg to front with jump, arms rise to 5th position, turn away in air from uplifted leg, land in first *arabesque*.
1−3	*Temps levé tombé*: (when working leg is already in air, *failli* becomes *temps levé tombé*).
4−6	*Fouetté sauté*.

Repeat sequence once more.

1−3	*Temps levé*, step through, step through.
4−6	*Grand jeté* (leg *croisé*), arms in second *arabesque*.
1−3	*Pas de bourrée couru*.

144

4–6	*Grand jeté.*
1–3	Two steps to *piqué* in second *arabesque* (preparation).
1–3	*Pas de bourrée couru* upstage on diagonal.
4–6	*Grand jeté en tournant*, arms rise to 5th position, open out at end of jump.

Repeat *couru* and *grand jeté en tournant.*

$\frac{4}{4}$ ♩ = 96

Allegro. *Petite batterie*: two *brisés en avant*, two *brisés en arrière*, three *entrechats-quatre*, one *royale*. Repeat on other side.

Counts

And–1	From 5th position, *brisé en avant*: open back leg to *effacé devant*, other leg beats back-front, arms in oppositional 4th position *devant*, body slightly turned toward front arm and leaning forward.

Repeat.

And–1	*Brisé en arrière*: open front leg to *effacé derrière*, arms in complementary 4th position, back arched.

Repeat.

And–1	*Entrechat-quatre*, arms in *bras bas.*

Repeat twice more.

And–4	*Royale.*

Repeat entire sequence on other side.

Grands battements.

Révérence.

VOCABULARY

As in the previous year, additions consist of using the vocabulary in a challenging fashion. Furthermore, the lesson becomes subject to outside influences, such as weather, student performing, and rehearsing schedules.

In the winter, muscles require a longer and slower warm-up period. Therefore, some *demi-pliés* and *tendus* or even a floor exercise can precede the traditional beginning of class. If students have a heavy rehearsing schedule the class can include fewer *fondus* and *développés* and use *pirouettes* instead of jumps in the *enchaînements*. If students are tired from a performance, a similarly less taxing lesson is applicable. No matter what the circumstance, students need to be impressed with the fact that they must not skip class because they are tired. If they aspire to a professional career, the daily lesson must be part of the routine of their day.

FOCUS AND EMPHASIS

In the final year of intensive study, all aspects of virtuosity will be explored. Virtuosity is demonstrated not only in the mastery of certain steps, such as *gargouillade*, *fouettés battus*, *tours de rein*, *brisés volés*, beaten combinations, and multiple turns, but also is manifest in the speed and accuracy of execution. Because the ability to move quickly and correctly from one pose into another is intimately linked to the dancer's understanding of weight transference, the teacher also needs to be aware of subtle changes in the dancer's alignment and make the appropriate corrections.

Virtuosity also relies on timing and creative phrasing. Both these concepts are usually described collectively as "musicality." In technical terms, musicality involves retarding or accelerating certain motions. It is instilled by teaching the child to hear the beat of the music, then the phrase, and to stay within the measure. It is rather like encouraging a first-grader to color within the lines of a drawing. Some people will argue that this process of limiting expressiveness kills creativity, but all art forms rely on a technique for execution and communication. When we learn to speak, we also learn the rules of the language.

As proficiency increases, the concept of musicality changes. The musical dancer develops an ability to use music to enhance movement, not merely to delineate it. It is no longer sufficient simply to stay within the rhythmic structure; one must interpret the music by cultivating a creative relationship between it and the movement, just as the painter fills a canvas with abstract shapes or the poet uses language in ways that move us and expand our perceptions. Musicality is most directly applicable to *allegro*, but it can be experienced in other sections of the lesson as well.

Barre

Execute a series of movements at varying speeds, like one slow *tendu* and two fast ones, or link a *frappé* exercise with *fondu*—four *frappés* and one *fondu en croix*. In this case there is an

Center

added dimension of contrast between percussive quality of the *frappé* and the flowing motion of the *fondu*.

Adagio.   Musicality is experienced not only by contrasting slow with fast or percussive with flowing, but also by holding some positions beyond the musical phrase and moving on the upbeat of the following phrase or, conversely, anticipating a new phrase by beginning the transition before the downbeat.

Allegro.   The same effect in *enchaînements* is achieved by using *glissade* or *pas de bourrée précipité* as transitional or preparatory steps. Preparations are quickened to allow more time for leaps and to add lightness to jumps.

Virtuosity is founded in all of the precepts honored through the years of training; the process of building a technique is relevant to its maintenance. A high level of proficiency is maintained when the minutest details of the technique are always part of the dancer's consciousness. The advanced student is already like the professional dancer, a fine-tuned instrument that needs expert care to keep it operating efficiently and beautifully. Health and efficiency are achieved only when misalignment and mannered execution are corrected before they cause any damage.

SAMPLE LESSON

Barre
$\frac{4}{4}$ ♩ = 76

Pliés.   One *grand plié*, one *demi-plié*, one rise to *demi-pointe*, *cambré* forward and back. In 2nd, 1st, 4th, and 5th positions.

Counts
1–4	*Grand plié* with first *port de bras*.
1–2	*Demi-plié*, bringing arm to 1st position.
3–4	*Relevé* to *demi-pointe*, sweeping arm outward to 2nd position *allongée*, with the upper back arched, head is turned and looking over the working arm.
1–4	*Cambré* forward, remaining on *demi-pointe*.
1–4	*Cambré* back, on the fourth count come down from *demi-pointe*, *pointe tendue* and close in 1st. Repeat in 1st, 4th, and 5th positions.

Repeat on the other side.

$\frac{4}{4}$ ♩ = 96

Battements tendus.   One *tendu* in two counts finishing in 5th position, *demi-plié* two fast *tendus*, executed to the front, side, and back, then four *tendus* to the side closing in 1st position with *port de bras*. Repeat beginning in the back.

Counts

1–2   *Tendu devant* from 5th position finishing in *demi-plié* in 5th, arm in 2nd.

And–3   *Tendu devant.*

And–4   *Tendu devant.* Repeat to side then back.

And–1   *Tendu* to side closing in 1st position, three times, the fourth closing in 5th back. Arm describes a *port de bras en dehors: Bras bas,* 1st position, 5th, then open to 2nd. The exercise is repeated from the back, the *port de bras is en dedans:* from 2nd to 5th through 1st, *bras bas* and finishes in 2nd.

$\frac{4}{4}$ ♩ = 100

Battements jetés.   Four *jetés* closing in 5th position; one *dégagé* to low *en l'air* position, brush through 5th to *demi-jambe,* brush through 5th to the extension *en l'air,* close in 5th. *En croix.* Arm is in 2nd position.

Counts

And–1   *Jeté devant* from 5th position to 5th.

Repeat for a total of four *jetés.*

And–1   *Dégagé* to 45 degrees *en l'air.*

And–2   Brush to *demi-jambe* position in front of the supporting leg.

And–3   Brush through 5th and open to the *en l'air* position.

And–4   Close in 5th. Repeat to the side, back, and side again.

Note: The first time to the side (following *devant*) the brush is in front of the supporting leg. The second time (following *derrière*) the brush is to *retiré derrière.*

$\frac{3}{4}$ ♩ = 138

Ronds de jambe par terre.   Two *ronds* in one measure each. Four *ronds* in double time. One *jeté arrondi* to *pointe tendue; cambré:* in deep 4th position, bending forward following *ronds en dehors,* and in *pointe tendue devant* bending back following *ronds en dedans.* Repeat entire sequence one more time, balance in low *arabesque* at the end.

Counts

1–3   From preparation to *pointe tendue à la seconde,* rond en dehors, arm in 2nd position.

1–3   *Rond en dehors.*

1–3   Two *ronds en dehors.*

1–3   Two *ronds en dehors.*

1–2   Brush through 1st position to low *attitude*

149

	devant, supporting leg in *demi-plié*, arm in 1st, and kick leg to a high *seconde*, arm rising to 2nd position *allongé*, head turned to the working arm, supporting leg straightens.
3	Lower leg to *pointe tendue derrière*, arm remains in 2nd position *allongé*.
1–3	Bend supporting leg, extend working leg to wide 4th toes fully pointed, bring arm to 5th.
1–3	Bend forward keeping arm in 5th.
1–3	Straighten body and supporting leg, arm remains in 5th.
1–3	Pass leg through 1st position to *pointe tendue devant* and repeat exercise *en dedans*. The timing for *cambré* back with the working foot in *pointe tendue devant* is the same as for the *cambré* in deep 4th. At the end, brush through 1st position and balance in low *arabesque*.

$\frac{3}{4}$ $\quad \downarrow = 132$

Battements fondus.   One *fondu double devant*; one *fondu double derrière* with the other leg, two *fondus à la seconde*; *demi-grand rond de jambe* to *devant* and *fouetté* into *arabesque*. Repeat on the other side then repeat beginning in the back, *demi-grand rond de jambe* to *derrière* and *fouetté* to *devant en l'air*.

Counts

1–6	From *dégagé* to *pointe tendue* in *seconde*, *fondu devant*. Arm, first *port de bras*.
1–3	Bring working leg to *retiré* position, supporting leg *demi-plié*.
1–3	*Relevé*, arm to 1st position.
1–6	Step onto working leg through 5th position (*coupé*) and *fondu derrière*, with other leg, arm in 2nd.
1–6	*Plié* and *relevé* in *retiré derrière*, arm in 5th.
1–6	*Coupé derrière* and *fondu* with the original working leg *à la seconde*, arm opens to 2nd.
1–6	*Fondu à la seconde*, arm first *port de bras*.
1–6	*Demi-grand rond de jambe* to *devant en l'air*, supporting leg *demi-plié*.
1–6	*Relevé* and *fouetté* into *arabesque* (turning toward the barre to face the other way); arm in 5th.
1–6	*Coupé derrière* and start the exercise on the other side.

Note: When reversing the sequence, the *fouetté* turns the body away from the barre to finish with the working leg extended *en l'air devant*.

$\frac{2}{4}$ ♩ = 112

Battements frappés.   Four *frappés à la seconde*; one *flic-flac en dehors en tournant*, one *flic-flac en dedans en tournant*. Repeat, starting *en dedans* then *en dehors*. Repeat on *demi-pointe* with *frappés doubles*.

Counts

And – 1   From a preparation to *pointe tendue seconde*, *frappé*, arm in 2nd.

Repeat for a total of four *frappés*.

And – 1   Brush back and front turning away from the barre *(en dehors)*.

And – 2   Finish *flic-flac* by extending to low *seconde*.

And – 1   Brush front then back turning toward the barre *(en dedans)*.

And – 2   Open to low *seconde*.

Repeat exercise reversing the *flic-flac*.

Repeat on *demi-pointe*.

Note: The supporting heel is lowered for the *flic-flac* to allow the working foot to brush the floor, so that the position is a very low *demi-pointe* during the turn; with the extension *à la seconde* the full *demi-pointe* is resumed.

$\frac{3}{4}$ ♩ = 144

Ronds de jambe en l'air.   Three *ronds en l'air en dehors*, *passé* to *devant en l'air*, supporting leg *demi-plié* (preparation), *fouetté en dehors* finishing in *attitude*; close in 5th position and reverse sequence finishing in *attitude devant*. Repeat on *demi-pointe*. Preparation: open leg to 90 degrees *en l'air*, arm in 2nd position.

Counts

1 – 3   Rond en dehors. Repeat for a total of three *ronds*.

1 – 3   *Passé* to *retiré* position, arm in 1st position.

1 – 3   *Développé devant*, *demi-plié* on supporting leg.

1 – 3   *Fouetté pirouette en dehors*.

1 – 3   Open to *attitude*, arm in 5th, staying on *demi-pointe*.

1 – 3   Extend leg then close in 5th, opening again to the side on the third count, arm in 2nd.

Repeat in reverse finishing with *fouetté pirouette en dedans* and *attitude devant*.

Repeat entire sequence on *demi-pointe* coming down to flat foot when the leg closes in 5th.

Note: In preparation for *fouetté en dedans*, the arm remains in 2nd position.

$$\frac{4}{4} \; \; \textbf{\textquotedbl} = 72$$

Adagio. *Développé* to *devant*, lower to *pointe tendue* and *cambré* forward over the leg, supporting leg *demi-plié*; raise the body and the leg at the same time while straightening the supporting leg; *Demi-plié* and *relevé* with a half turn away from the barre (*en dehors*) keeping the working leg extended *devant*; *balancé* through 1st position to *arabesque*, supporting leg *demi-plié*; straighten supporting leg while doing a *cambré* back, the working leg is still fully extended in *arabesque*; *demi-plié* and *relevé* with a half-turn toward the barre (*en dehors*) bringing working leg to a high *retiré* position. Repeat one more time then repeat on the other side.

Counts

1−4	From 5th position, *développé devant* opening arm to 2nd.
1−4	Bring arm to 5th while the supporting leg bends, the working leg lowers to *pointe tendue* and the body bends forward.
1−4	Keeping arm in 5th, straighten supporting leg while body returns to vertical, bringing the working leg up at the same time.
1−4	*Demi-plié* and *relevé* keeping the working leg extended while the body turns to the other side, the new working arm is in 5th; the position is *effacé*.
1−4	Coming down from the *demi-pointe*, *balancé* through 1st position to *arabesque* with *demi-plié* on supporting leg, arm in *allongé devant*.
1−4	Straighten supporting leg while the arm rises to 5th and the body bends back, the *arabesque* is maintained, arm in 5th.
1−4	Return to vertical, *demi-plié* and *relevé* with a half-turn toward the barre, bringing working leg to a high *retiré* position, arm in 5th.
1−4	Hold position.

Repeat entire sequence.

Repeat on other side.

Note: This exercise can also be done with opposite *cambrés*: the body bends back when the leg is extended to the

$\frac{4}{4}$ ♩ = 120

front, the leg in this case stays in the extension; then with the *arabesque*, a *penché* takes the place of the *cambré*.

Petits battements sur le cou-de-pied. Four *petits battements* ending on *demi-plié* with working leg in *demi-jambe* position; *pirouette en dehors, demi-plié, pirouette en dehors* finishing on *demi-pointe* and eight *petits battements à demi-jambe*. Repeat sequence four times. Preparation: *pointe tendue à la seconde*.

Counts

1−4	*Petits battements*, arm in *bras bas*.
And	*Demi-plié* on supporting leg, working leg in *demi-jambe*, arm in 1st position.
1−2	*Pirouette en dehors*, finishing on *demi-pointe*, arm in 1st.
And	*Demi-plié*.
3−4	*Pirouette*, finishing on *demi-pointe*.
1−4	*Petits battements à demi-jambe*, arm returns to *bras bas*.
And	Lower supporting heel.

Repeat sequence for a total of four times.

$\frac{4}{4}$ ♩ = 96

Grands battements. One *grand battement*, closing in 5th position, one *battement développé*, one *battement enveloppé*, and one *battement* closing in 5th. *En croix.*

Counts

And−1	From 5th position *grand battement devant*, arm in 5th.
And−2	Passing quickly through *retiré: battement développé*.
And−3	*Battement*, then enfold the leg passing through *retiré* before closing in 5th.
And−4	*Grand battement*.
And−1	Open arm to 2nd.
And−1	Repeat to the side, then to the back with the arm in *allongé devant*, and to the side again with arm in 2nd.

Center
$\frac{3}{4}$ ♩ = 69

Port de bras. *Chassé en avant, fondu derrière; chassé de côté, fondu à la seconde, chassé en arrière, fondu devant, demi-plié* and *fouetté en dedans* from the *devant* extension to second *arabesque*, place the back leg in 4th position and *pirouettes en dehors, pas de basque en avant, pas de basque en avant en tournant, pas de basque en avant* into 4th position and *pirouettes fouettés en dedans, changement*. Repeat on other side.

153

Counts

1 – 3   From 5th position *chassé en avant* to *pointe tendue croisée derrière*, arms in oppositional 4th position.

1 – 3   Begin *fondu*, *demi-plié* on supporting leg bringing working leg to *demi-jambe derrière*, arms lower to *bras bas*.

1 – 3   Leg unfolds to *derrière en l'air* position, arms rise to oppositional 4th position.

1 – 3   Rise to *demi-pointe* and close in 5th back still on *demi-pointe*, then lower heels and arms to 2nd.

1 – 3   *Chassé de côté* with the front leg to *pointe tendue* in *seconde*, arms in 2nd.

1 – 3   Same timing as for *derrière*: *fondu* with the working leg, arms first *port de bras*, rise, then close in front.

1 – 3   *Chassé en arrière* to *pointe tendue croisée devant*, arms in oppositional 4th position.

1 – 3   Begin *fondu*, arms *port de bras* as before.

1 – 3   Unfold leg, arms in oppositional 4th position.

1 – 3   *Demi-plié* on supporting leg, leg and arms remain in position.

1 – 3   *Relevé* on supporting leg as the body turns away from the leg, the other arm comes to 5th position for the oppositional 4th position on the other side, finish in *derrière en l'air croisé*, arms in oppositional 4th position (*fouetté en dedans*).

1 – 3   Place back leg into 4th position as preparation, arms in oppositional 4th position *devant*.

1 – 3   *Pirouettes en dehors* finishing in 5th position back.

1 – 3   *Pas de basque en avant*, finish by closing 5th position back.

1 – 3   *Pas de basque en avant en tournant*: the action is the same as for regular *pas de basque* with the addition of a quarter-turn away from the working leg as it opens from *devant à la seconde* (the body now faces the upstage corner), then as the working leg passes through 1st position, the swivel is completed with the *chassé en avant to pointe tendue derrière*, close in 5th position back.

1–3	*Pas de basque en avant* into 4th position. Preparation: arms in complementary 4th position *devant*.
1–3	*Pirouettes fouettés en dedans*, arms in 5th, finish in 5th position front.
1–3	Little *changement*.

Repeat sequence on other side.

$\frac{4}{4}$ ♩ = 104

Battements tendus. One *tendu devant croisé*, one *tendu derrière croisé*, two *tendus dessous à la seconde* (alternate legs), *tombé pirouette piqué en dehors* finishing in *arabesque croisée* and *relevé en tournant* bringing working leg to *retiré*, repeat *pirouette* combination twice more closing the last one in 5th position back. Repeat to the other side.

Counts

1–2	From 5th position, *tendu croisé devant*, arms in oppositional 4th position; close in 5th position.
3–4	*Tendu derrière croisé* (with the other leg), arms remain; close in 5th position.
1–2	*Tendu à la seconde* with front leg closing in the back, arms in 2nd position.
3–4	*Tendu à la seconde* with the other leg.
And–1	*Tombé* to *effacé*, *piqué* to *pirouette en dehors*.
2	Finish in *arabesque croisée*, *demi-plié* on supporting leg.
3–4	*Relevé* to *pirouette en dehors* bringing the working leg to *retiré* position.
And–1	*Tombé* from the *retiré* position and repeat sequence of *pirouettes*, the last one closing in 5th position back.

Repeat to the other side.

$\frac{3}{4}$ ♩ = 132

Ronds de jambe en l'air. Three *ronds de jambe en dehors*, *passé* to *retiré* and *développé effacé devant*, *demi-plié* and *piqué* into *arabesque*. Return the body to *en face* placing leg in *seconde en l'air*, three *ronds en dedans*, *passé* to *arabesque croisée* (preparation: arms in complementary 4th position). *Demi-plié* on supporting leg and *fouetté pirouette en attitude devant en dedans*. Finish the turn with a *demi-plié* on the supporting leg and *relevé* extending working leg to *croisé devant*, *tombé* into a wide 4th position, *pas de bourrée en tournant en dehors*, closing in 5th position, little *glissade de côté changée*. Repeat to the other side.

Counts

| 1–3 | From 5th position, front leg *à la seconde en l'air*, arms in 2nd. |

1 – 3   *Rond en dehors.*

Repeat for a total of three *ronds* (the *ronds* can also be performed on *demi-pointe*).

1 – 3   *Passé* to a high *retiré* position.

1 – 3   *Développé effacé devant*, supporting leg *demi-plié*, arms in oppositional 4th position.

1 – 3   *Piqué* to first *arabesque*, arms in complementary *allongé*.

1 – 3   With a little *relevé* to *demi-pointe*, keeping working leg straight, return *à la seconde*, arms in 2nd position.

1 – 3   *Ronds en dedans.*

Repeat for a total of three *ronds*.

1 – 3   *Passé* to high *retiré*, arms in 1st position.

1 – 3   *Développé* to *croisée derrière en l'air*, *demi-plié* on supporting leg, arms in complementary 4th position *devant*.

1 – 3   Whip the leg to *attitude devant* with *relevé*, arms are in oppositional 3rd position during the turn.

1 – 3   Finish the *pirouette* with *demi-plié* and quick *relevé*, extending the leg *devant*, arms in 3rd position *allongé*, body arched back slightly.

1 – 3   *Tombé* onto the working leg, arms opening to 2nd position, *pas de bourrée dessous en tournant* finishing in 5th position and little *glissade de côté changée*.

Repeat on the other side.

The following combination is especially suitable for men. If it is included in this lesson, the *port de bras* exercise should not be performed, but another version omitting the *fondu* substituted.

$\frac{4}{4}$ ♩ = 69
Tango

Battements fondus with grandes pirouettes.   One *fondu* to *croisé devant en l'air*, *tombé* to 4th position, *pirouettes en dedans en attitude* finishing in *attitude effacée*, *fondu à la derrière effacé*, *fondu à la seconde en face*, *demi-plié* and *piqué* lifting other leg *à la seconde*, *demi-plié* and *pas de bourrée dessous* to 4th position *croisé*, *pirouettes* in *seconde en dedans*, *demi-plié*, *pirouettes* in *arabesque en dedans*, *soutenu en tournant* finishing with a *retiré passé*, close in 5th position back.

Counts

1 – 3   From 5th position, *fondu devant*, arms in

oppositional 4th position, *tombé* into 4th position; front leg *demi-plié*, arms in complementary 4th position *devant*.

1 – 4   *Pirouettes en dedans* in *attitude*, end in *effacé*, arms remain.

1 – 4   *Fondu derrière effacé*, arms *port de bras* to finish in 2nd position *arabesque*.

1 – 4   *Fondu à la seconde en face*, arms open to 2nd position.

1   *Demi-plié* on supporting leg keeping the other in *seconde*.

2   *Piqué* onto the working leg, lifting the other to *seconde*.

3 – 4   *Demi-plié* keeping the leg in *seconde* then *pas de bourrée dessous* finishing in 4th position *croisé*, *demi-plié* on front leg, arms in complementary 4th position *devant*.

1 – 4   *Pirouette en dedans* in *seconde*, arms in 5th position.

1 – 4   *Demi-plié* and *relevé* immediately into first *arabesque*, continuing to turn.

1 – 4   *Demi-plié* on supporting leg then bring the working leg to 5th position in front for the *soutenu en tournant*. Before the turn is completed raise the front leg to *retiré*, arms in 5th, close in 5th position back.

Repeat to the other side.

Note: The *soutenu* to *retiré* can also be interpreted as a *piqué pirouette en dehors*. The action is the same except the 5th position at the beginning of the *soutenu* is omitted; instead the weight is placed straightaway on the new supporting leg, the other rising to *retiré*.

$\frac{4}{4}$ ♩ = 66

Adagio.   *Grand plié* in 5th position, arms in complementary 4th position *devant*. From the depth of the *plié* begin *pirouette en dehors* finishing in *attitude croisée devant*. *Grand rond de jambe en dehors* finishing in first *arabesque croisée*. *Promenade en dehors* bringing the working leg to a high *retiré* and *développé croisé devant*. *Tombé, coupé, renversé en dehors*, finishing with *pas de bourée en tournant en dehors* closing in 5th position. *Développé* with the back leg to *écarté derrière*, *renversé en dedans* finishing in *seconde en face*, with *demi-plié* and *relevé* and turn to first *arabesque*, *penché* in *arabesque*, *tombé* to 4th position *croisé* and *pirouettes en dehors* raising the arms to 5th position on the last turn and finishing in a deep 4th position, arms in first *arabesque croisée*.

Counts

1—4   From 5th position, arms in 2nd, *grand plié* lowering the arms to *bras bas* then lifting to complementary 4th position *devant*.

1—4   From the depth of the *plié*, rise into a *pirouette en dehors* finishing in *attitude devant*, arms in oppositional 4th position.

1—4   Extend working leg, begin *grand round de jambe* passing through *seconde*, arms in 2nd position.

1—4   Continue *rond* finishing in first *arabesque croisée*.

1—4   *Promenade en dehors* (toward the working leg) bringing working leg to high *retiré*, arms in 1st position.

1—4   *Développé croisé devant* rising on *demi-pointe*, arms in oppositional 4th position.

And   *Tombé, coupé dessous*, the body leaning over the front leg which is in *demi-plié*, arms in complementary 4th position *devant*.

1—3   *Renversé*: Lift front leg to *devant*, other leg on *demi-pointe*, working leg travels through *seconde* to *attitude*, the front arm opens to 2nd position then lift to 5th as the leg reaches *attitude*. The final position is with the body tilted forward and the back strongly arched.

4   *Pas de bourrée dessous en tournant*, finish in 5th position *enface*, arms *bras bas*.

Note: The *renversé* is done from *croisé devant* to *attitude croisée*, then the *pas de bourrée* is turned.

1—4   *Développé* to *écarté derrière*, arms in oppositional 4th position.

1—2   *Renversé en dedans*: Bring the working leg to a very high *retiré*, bending the body sideways toward the working leg, the supporting leg *demi-plié*, arms in 1st position. Turn in this position then open working leg *à la seconde* with a *relevé* on the supporting leg, arms open to a low 2nd position, palms out.

3—4   *Demi-plié*, return the body to upright, and quickly *relevé* into first *arabesque (fouetté* into *arabesque)*.

1 – 2	Lower supporting heel and begin *penché*.
3 – 4	Continue *penché*.
1 – 4	Reach the depth of the *penché* and hold position.
1 – 8	Return to upright.
1 – 4	*Relevé* to *demi-pointe*, *tombé* to 4th position *croisé*, arms in oppositional 4th position *devant*.
1 – 4	*Pointe tendue* back leg then replace the heel on the floor, front arm *allongé*, then return to *devant*.
1 – 4	*Pirouettes en dehors*, arms in 1st position then raise arms to 5th on the last *pirouette* (the spins are continuous, no *demi-plié relevé* when the arms are raised).
1 – 4	Finish in deep 4th position (working leg in the back), arms in *allongé*, first *arabesque croisée*.

Repeat on the other side.

$\frac{4}{4}$ $\downarrow$ = 104

Allegro. Four *changements*, one *entrechat-trois dessous*, two *petits jetés dessus*, *temps levé en tournant en dehors*, end with *tombé en avant*, *coupé dessous* and *gargouillade*, *pas de chat*, *temps de cuisses*, *sissonne de côté dessous*, *entrechat-quatre*. Repeat on the other side.

Counts

And – 4	*Changements*, arms *bras bas*.
And – 1	*Entrechat-trois dessous*: front leg beats front and finishes in *demi-jambe derrière*, arms complementary 4th position *devant*.
And – 3	Two *petits jetés dessus*, arms changing to complementary 4th position *devant* with each *jeté*.
And – 4	*Temps levé en tournant en dedans*, working leg passes to the front, *tombé en avant*.
And – 1	*Coupé* with the back leg, arms in complementary 4th position *devant*.
And – 2	*Gargouillade*: Front leg, open to 45-degree *seconde*, does a quick *double rond de jambe en l'air en dehors*. The supporting leg pushes off and also does a *double rond en dedans* and closes in 5th position front (the second *rond de jambe* is completed after the landing has occurred on the other leg, the second leg stretches fully before closing), arms open to 2nd position.

And — 3   *Pas de chat*, arms in oppositional 4th position *devant*.

And — 4   *Temps de cuisses*, bringing the back foot to the front, arms remain.

And — 1   *Sissonne de côté dessous*, front leg closes back, arms change to complementary 4th position *devant*.

And — 2   *Entrechat quatre*, arms in *bras bas*:

And — 4   Hold.

Repeat on the other side.

$\frac{3}{4}$ ♩ = 176

Allegro.   *Failli fouetté sauté battu* finishing in first *arabesque, temps levé tombé, coupé dessous* and *cabriole croisée devant, tombé, pas de bourrée dessous en tournant, rond de jambe sauté* finishing in 5th position, *glissade sans changer, assemblé dessus*. Although many of these steps are from the *grand allegro* vocabulary in this *enchaînement*, they are not performed to their full height. The sequence is danced to a fairly fast waltz from one corner to the other and later repeated on the other side.

Counts

1 — 3   From 5th position, *failli*, arms to 1st position.

1 — 3   *Fouetté sauté*: from the 4th position the back leg kicks front as the push off occurs. The second leg beats the back of the front leg which remains in full extension, then the body turns away from the leg leaving it in first *arabesque* as the landing occurs. The arms rise to 5th position then lower to first *arabesque*.

1 — 3   *Temps levé tombé*, spring up with the leg still in *arabesque* then *tombé* onto the working leg to 4th position front, arms meet in 1st position.

1 — 3   *Coupé* with the back leg and *cabriole croisée* devant, arms in complementary 4th position.

1 — 3   *Pas de bourrée dessous en tournant:* turn toward the back leg, arms in 1st, finish in 5th position.

1 — 3   *Rond de jambe sauté*: open the back leg *à la seconde* with the push off, two *ronds en dedans* while in the air, close in 5th position front, arms in 2nd position.

1 — 3   *Glissade* with the back leg without changing feet, arms remain in 2nd.

1 — 3   *Assemblé dessus*, back leg closes in 5th position front, arms lower to *bras bas*.

$\frac{3}{4}$ ♩ = 168

Repeat on the same side.

Allegro. From the corner on a diagonal: *Pas de bourrée couru*; *grand jeté* with the *croisé* leg, repeated three times; two steps into *piqué* to second *arabesque croisée*. Traveling upstage *pas de bourrée couru*; *grand jeté en tournant* repeated three times. Finish the last *jeté* with *pas de bourrée dessous en tournant* and extend front leg to *pointe tendue croisée devant*. Two measures of *chaînés*; two *piqués pirouettes en dehors* into four *fouettés en tournant*. Repeat the *chaînés pirouettes* and *fouettés* sequence then *chaînés* to the corner to end. Preparation: *dégagé* to *pointe tendue croisée*. For men, instead of the turns sequence: *temps levé tombé pas de bourrée* to 4th position preparation, *pirouettes en dehors* into *seconde*, *petits sautés* in *seconde* finishing by pulling into *pirouettes en dehors* then *chaînés* to the corner.

Counts

1−3	*Pas de bourrée couru*, arms come from 2nd position through *bras bas* to 1st position.
1−3	*Grand jeté* with the *croisé* leg, arms opening to low 2nd position palms up.

Repeat for a total of three times.

1−3	Step through onto the working leg then *piqué* into second *arabesque*, arms in oppositional 4th position.
1−3	*Pas de bourrée couru* upstage, arms passing through *bras bas* to 1st.
1−3	*Grand jeté en tournant*, arms rising to 5th position and opening to 2nd as the landing occurs.

Repeat for a total of three times.

1−3	*Pas de bourrée dessous en tournant*, then *dégagé* front leg to *pointe tendue croisée devant*, arms in complementary 4th position *devant*.
1−6	*Chaînés*, arms in 1st.
1−3	*Tombé* and *piqué* into *pirouette en dehors*.
1−3	*Tombé*, *piqué* to *pirouette en dehors* (arms are in 1st for the turn and open to 2nd with the *tombé*). Finish the turn with *développé* to *devant*, supporting leg on *demi-plié* (the position is *en face*).
1−3	*Fouetté en dehors*.

Repeat for a total of four *fouettés*.

Repeat *chaînés*, *piqué pirouette*, *fouettés* sequence one more time then *chaînés* to the corner to finish.

161

Ending sequence for men:

1 – 3   *Temps levé, tombé* onto front leg traveling on a diagonal, *pas de bourrée dessous* finishing in 4th position preparation.

1 – 3   *Pirouettes en dehors* finishing with a *développé à la seconde*, arms in 2nd position, *demi-plié* on supporting leg.

1 – 3   *Petits sautés* in *seconde*, arms remain in 2nd.

Continue *petits sautés* for a total of twelve measures, then pull in the working leg into *retiré* position for *pirouettes en dehors*. Finish in 4th position or with *chaînés* to the corner.

Note: In both versions, the final *chaînés* are tagged on after the sixty-four measures of the *enchaînément* are concluded.

$\frac{6}{8}$ $\sqrt{.} = 96$

Allegro.   Eight *brisés volés, pas de bourrée en tournant en dehors, sous-sus*, two *entrechat-six*. Repeat on the same side.

Counts

And – 1   From 5th position *brisé volé*: open the back leg and landing on it after the beat with the second leg extended *en l'air devant*.

And – 2   *Brisé volé* back, finishing with the first leg extended in low *en l'air derrière* position. Repeat for a total of eight *brisés*.

And – 1   *Pas de bourrée dessous en tournant en dehors*, finishing in 5th position, arms lower to *bras bas*.

And – 2   *Sous-sus*, arms open to 2nd.

And – 1   *Entrechat-six*, arms lift to high 2nd position *allongé*.

And – 2   *Entrechat-six*.

Repeat to the same side on a diagonal.

Grands battements.

Révérence.

CONCLUSION

Each of the years discussed in this book is significant to acquiring classical technique. The introduction of new material keeps pace with students' physical development and intellectual understanding, which avoids the problem of introducing new material too rapidly.

Dance training is a very conservative form of education that fosters commitment, steadfastness, effort, and concentration. Constant vigilance must be exercised to keep mannerisms from creeping into execution of the movements. There are no shortcuts in the acquisition of pure classical line. There was a very popular teacher in London who, it was reputed, could teach anyone to balance on *demi-pointe*. The half-joking secret was, if your right leg was up, you need only contract your left earlobe to stay forever suspended. Unfortunately, there is no panacea that will enable dancers to find an unerring equilibrium or give them the ability to perform twelve *pirouettes*.

In classical dance we spend long years practicing movements and poses that will eventually enable us to move freely within the parameters of the art form. In the early years of training we acquire the fundamental movement habits of that form, which build the needed musculature to perform the steps. In that respect, we are both the violin maker and the violin.

Bad habits that develop during training usually spring from a less than ideal physique or a too rapid progression. Both problems ultimately have the same effect—harmonious and stylistically correct movement is difficult if not impossible to achieve because unwanted musculature is developed through misdirected effort, the tensile strength of the muscles pulls the skeletal alignment off center, and new compensations are born from the additional effort of keeping upright. If muscles are capable of pulling the skeletal structure out of alignment, they can also be trained to correct ungainly posture. A child with less than ideal physique will find the technique harder to execute, but with perseverance can overcome many problems.

However, along with the emphasis on alignment and placement, the ultimate purpose of a well-grounded technique must not be forgotten—freedom of motion, the ability to move with optimum grace and efficiency. In that respect classical training transcends its own style. Ironically, but not accidentally, those dancers who are most deeply steeped in the classical tradition are the most successful in their exploration of other idioms.

Through the years of training, the focus gradually shifts from perfecting unfamiliar steps to a clear understanding of the mechanics of the steps and an appreciation of the physical responses to these demands. With this understanding, the dancer is able to make subtle adjustments and apply efficiently the effort inherent in any motion, thereby becoming a sensitive interpreter.

Recently, I received a bouquet of daisies from one of my students. On the note accompanying the flowers she wrote: "When I was a child I had the notion that daisies were stars that had become flowers."

I wish you many daisies in your garden.

GLOSSARY

Adagio. Slow movements. Refers to high extensions as well as a section of the lesson in the center. It is also used to describe a partnered dance. Vocabulary for *adagio* at the *barre* includes *battement relevé*, *développé*, *grand rond de jambe*, *grand fouetté*, *penché* and *allongé* positions, and *cambré*.

Air, en l'. *See* Directions

Allegro. Light or springy movements, such as leaps or skips.

Allongé. "Laid out." Describes any position of the arms when the palms are turned face downward. All *arabesques* use *allongé* positioning.

Second position allongé. Arms in 2nd position, downstage arm angled upward and slightly behind the shoulder, upstage arm straight out from the shoulder. This position can include a slight uplift of the upper back, which gives it a very broad and open look, rather like the statues on the prow of old ships with chest thrust forward.

Third position allongé. Both arms in front of the body, upstage arm angled upward, downstage arm straight out from the shoulder.

Arabesque. "Ornament." The name is thought to be derived from descriptions of intricate Moorish designs. Classified as a "big pose." A 90-degree, or higher, extension of one straight leg to the back, arms in various *allongé* positions.

First arabesque. A complementary pose, the same arm as the front leg is extended forward in *allongé*, the other arm is in 2nd position when the pose is first learned, later it opens out to create the long line (from tip of fingers of front arm to tip of fingers of back arm) characteristic of the position.

Second arabesque. An oppositional pose, the arm opposite to the front leg is extended forward, the other arm is in 2nd position. Both are in *allongé*.

Note: Both first and second *arabesques* can also be qualified as *ouvertes*—open in relation to the audience.

First arabesque croisée. Arms as in arabesque *ouverte*, but the leg is in a crossed-over position in relation to the audience; the body spirals, the back is strongly arched in order to create a complementary line between arms and leg.

Second arabesque croisée. Arms as in *arabesque ouverte*, but the leg is in a crossed-over position in relation to the audience.

Arabesque allongée. Laid-out or lengthened *arabesque*. The line to be achieved is parallel to the floor, arms and extended leg on the same plane; the body leans forward but the leg remains at 90 degrees.

Arabesque penchée. Tilted *arabesque*. The leg is lifted as high as it can go and the body is tilted forward commensurately; the back is strongly arched.

Arrière, en. *See* Directions

Assemblé. "To put together or assemble." A jump from one foot onto two. The working leg opens to 45 degrees *en l'air*, the supporting leg pushes off the floor, the legs come together before landing in 5th position.

Assemblé dessous. *Assemblé* "under." From 5th position, the front leg opens to the side and closes in the back at the conclusion of the jump. When executed in a series with alternating legs it is also called *en montant*.

Assemblé dessus. *Assemblé* "over." From 5th position, the back leg opens to the side and closes in front at the conclusion of the jump. When executed in a series with alternating legs it is also called *en descendant*.

Note: Both versions of the *assemblé* are done without traveling from side to side, only forward and back, and that only by virtue of closing one leg in front of or in back of the other.

Assemblé derrière. *Assemblé* "to the back." The back leg opens to 45 degrees, the supporting leg pushes off the floor; the landing is on both legs, the back leg closing in 5th position back.

Assemblé devant. *Assemblé* "to the front." The front leg opens to the front, and the landing occurs on both legs, the front leg closing in front.

Assemblé volé. "Flying" *assemblé*. Usually preceded by a *failli*, the back leg opens to 90 degrees in *écarté devant* position, arms in *seconde allongée*. The jump travels forward on a diagonal, the working leg closing front at the completion of the jump.

Assemblé en tournant. *Assemblé* with a revolution of the body in the air ("turning"). Usually preceded by a *pas de bourrée couru* toward an upstage corner, the working leg opens front to 90 degrees, the legs meet in the air while the body revolves one-and-a-half times, finishing in 5th position, working leg in front, facing toward the front. The arms are held in 2nd position during the *pas de bourrée*, then pass through *bras bas*, 1st

164

position, and reaching 5th position as the revolution begins. They return to 2nd position only after the landing has occurred.

Assemblé sur les pointes. *Assemblé* onto *pointe.* *Assemblés dessous, dessus, derrière,* and *devant* can all be performed on *pointe.* The execution is the same as for *assemblé sauté,* but instead of jumping, the push-off lands on *pointe.*

Attitude. "Pose." This position was named by Carlo Blasis and inspired by the statue of Mercury by Giovanni da Bologna. One leg is lifted in the back to 90 degrees and bent at the knee. The arms are in 4th position in opposition to the front leg. This pose is executed both in *croisé* and in *effacé.* If in *croisé,* the same arm as the front leg is in 5th position and the position becomes *épaulé.*

Attitude devant. *Attitude* "to the front." The leg is raised in front, bent at the knee and the lower leg angled downward. The arms are in 4th position in opposition to the front leg. Generally executed in a *croisé* position. Can also be done in a complementary fashion with the same arm raised as the front leg.

Avant, en. *See* Directions

Balancé. "See-saw." A rocking motion. A step in three counts resembling a waltz. One: step out to the side into *demi-plié,* the other leg on the *cou-de-pied derrière.* Two: rise on *demi-pointe* onto the back leg, the other leg on the *cou-de-pied devant.* Three: return onto the front leg in *demi-plié.* The movement is then repeated to the other side.

Balancé with battement jeté or grand battement. The working leg is raised alternately front and back, passing through 1st position. With *battement jeté* the leg rises to 45 degrees only and the body remains upright. With *grand battement* the leg rises to 90 degrees or above and the body rocks forward and back responding to the movement of the leg.

Ballonné. "Bounce, like a ball." Usually preceded by a *coupé,* the working leg opens to the side in a strong *battement* to 90 degrees. The supporting leg pushes off the floor and the landing is onto the supporting leg, the working leg bending in to a *demi-jambe* position. Is also executed to the front and the back.

Ballonné dessous. *Coupé* with the back leg, the front leg opening to the side and returning to *demi-jambe derrière* at the conclusion of the jump.

Ballonné dessus. The front leg executes the *coupé,* the back leg opens to the side and comes to *demi-jambe devant* position at the conclusion of the jump.

Ballonné derrière. Usually executed as a series. The back leg opens to the back and comes to *demi-jambe* position back at the conclusion of the jump. Then the push off occurs again with the working leg extending to the back and again returning to *demi-jambe* as the landing occurs. The step travels slightly backward with each jumped extension.

Ballonné devant. The same as *derrière* except that the leg opens to the front and the step travels forward.

Ballonné sur les pointes. *Dessous* and *dessus:* the *coupé,* instead of leading into a jump, results in a *piqué* onto *pointe* the working leg opening to the side. The movement finishes in *demi-plié* on the supporting leg, the working leg in *demi-jambe* position. *Derrière* and *devant:* in a series, extend the leg out with a *relevé* onto *pointe* and bring it back to *demi-jambe* position with the *demi-plié.*

Ballotté. "Rocked from side to side, like a boat on waves." There are two versions of this step. Both are usually performed in an *effacé* position.

Italian. The back leg is lifted to a high *retiré derrière.* With a spring, the other leg comes up into *retiré devant,* finishing with a *développé effacé devant.* As the landing occurs on the back leg, the body is tilted back, arms in 4th position *devant* (the same arm as the landing leg is in front, oppositional position). With a spring, the extended leg is brought to *retiré,* the supporting leg also comes to *retiré* (both feet are off the floor). The landing occurs on the front leg, the back leg extended *derrière,* the body tilting forward, the same arm as the landing leg is in front (complementary position). The movement is repeated.

Note: The head is over the front shoulder when the front leg is extended and looks over the front arm when the back leg is extended. The extension can be emphasized, in which case the movement is performed quite slowly. The *ballotté* can also be done at a faster speed, in which case the legs do not need to extend above 90 degrees.

Russian. The same rocking motion is performed, but with straight legs. The back leg extends to a low *en l'air* position *derrière,* as the spring off the floor occurs, the two legs meet in the air, the landing occurs on the back leg the front extended in a low *devant* position. The movement is repeated. The arms and head positions are as above.

Basque, pas de. A composite step of Basque origin, formerly called *pas de Russe.* It includes a *dégagé,* a *demi-rond de jambe par terre,* and a *chassé.*

En avant. *Dégagé* to *pointe tendue devant* with the front leg, the supporting leg is in *demi-plié*, arms are in 1st position. *Demi-rond de jambe à la seconde*, supporting leg still in *demi-plié*, the arms open to 2nd position. Weight is tranferred onto the working leg, which bends in a *demi-plié* while the other leg extends to *pointe tendue* in *seconde*. This leg then slides through 1st position, both legs in *demi-plié*, arms coming through *bras bas* and 1st position to open forward as the leg continues to slide forward through 4th position. The movement ends in a *pointe tendue derrière*, before closing in 5th position.

En arrière. The movement reverses with *dégagé derrière*, *demi-rond de jambe en dedans*, transferring weight onto the original working leg, then through 1st position *chassé en arrière* to finish with *pointe tendue devant*. The arms are the same as the *en avant* version.

Pas de basque de côté. This version omits the *rond de jambe*, opening directly to the side, when the weight is transferred onto the original working leg. The other leg passes through a low *retiré* position before stepping forward, the other leg extended in *pointe tendue*. *En avant*: from 5th position, the front leg extends to a low *en l'air* position to the side. Transfer weight onto it, the second leg passes through a *retiré* and steps forward, the original working leg extends in *pointe tendue derrière*. *En arrière*: the back leg extends to the side and takes the weight, the second leg steps back, the original working leg extends to *pointe tendue devant*.

Basque, saut de. *Pas de basque* performed with jumps.

Petit. With a little jump at the moment of transfer from one leg to the other and as the leg passes through *retiré*.

En tournant. Usually preceded by a *pas de bourrée couru* or a *chassé*: the working leg extends with a strong *battement* to *devant en l'air* position, the arms are in 1st position. At the moment of the extension the other leg pushes off the floor, then comes to a high *retiré* position as the body revolves in the air, the arms in 5th position during the turn. The landing occurs in the same position (*retiré*) as was assumed for the turn. The step can be repeated again beginning with the preparatory *couru* or *chassé*.

Battement. "Beating." Refers to a number of movements that include a beating action of the leg. The various types of battements make up most of the exercises performed *à la barre*. See *Fouetté, Rond de jambe*.

Battement fondu. "Melting." An extension through a *développé* of the working leg, while the supporting leg bends then straightens. The motion of the two legs is synchronized so that both bend, the working leg raised to a *demi-jambe* position, the supporting leg in *demi-plié*; then both straighten, the working leg into an extension and the supporting leg to a straight knee.

Battement fondu double. After the initial extension is performed, the working leg returns to *demi-jambe* and a *relevé* in the *retiré* position is executed.

Battement frappé. "To hit or strike." A strong movement with the accent out from a *cou-de-pied* position to an extension at 45 degrees, then the working leg returns to *cou-de-pied* to start the next *frappé*.

Battement frappé double. "Beaten *frappé*." The working leg beats front-back or back-front before extending into the open position.

Battement jeté. "Thrown beating." The working leg opens to a height of 45 degrees, fully stretched, then returns to the closed position.

Battement jeté piqué. A jabbing, bouncing action of a fully pointed foot, touching then lifting off the floor.

Battement raccourci. "To foreshorten." Often performed in the same sequence as *battement frappé*. The working leg, from an extended position, comes in to a *demi-jambe* position with a strong accent in. The foot remains fully pointed.

Battement relevé. "To lift or raise." *Dégagé* to *pointe tendue*, then the straight leg is lifted to 90 degrees or higher; pass through *pointe tendue* before closing in 5th position. The movement can be done in all directions.

Battement tendu. "Stretched beating." The working leg extends outward until the toes are fully stretched and then returns to the closed position. The toes are never allowed to lose contact with the floor.

Petit battement sur le cou-de-pied. "Little beating." The working foot is wrapped around the ankle, just above the ankle bone: with the position in front, the heel touches the ankle and the toes touch the back of the supporting heel. With the position in back, the heel touches the back of the supporting ankle and the toes wing-away from the supporting leg. The working foot is slightly flexed at the ankle but the instep is fully contracted. During the movement, the thigh is held in a turned-out position while the lower leg (from the knee) opens slightly to allow the working foot to bypass the supporting leg as it strikes alternately front and back.

Petit battement à demi-jambe. In this version, the foot is fully stretched and the leg lifted so that the toes touch the supporting leg at the height of the calf. As with the previous version, the thigh is held immobile while the toes of the working leg beat front and back.

Petit battement battu. This movement beats either front or back and is generally performed on *demi-pointe* accompanied by the second *port de bras* (*en dehors* when the foot beats in front, *en dedans* when the foot beats in the back). For the beating in front, the foot is fully stretched, the leg opens slightly outward from the knee and beats-in in rapid succession. For the beating in the back, the foot is winged, only the heel touching the supporting ankle, the action of the successive beats takes the working foot away (toward the back) and brings the foot again to the supporting ankle.

Petit battement par terre. This movement is performed with a preparatory opening to 45 degrees to the side. The leg then comes back to 5th position front without putting any weight on it. It opens enough to bypass the supporting leg and slides to the back, then opens to the *en l'air* position. The movement is then repeated, beating back-front this time. The timing for the movement is "And," beating front-back; "One," opening to the extension; "And," beating back-front; "One," opening to the extension.

Grand battement. "Big beating." From 5th position, the working leg is thrown into a high extension and returns to 5th position. The *battement* can be performed in all directions.

Note: For greater detail in executing all movements of the barre, their intent and relationship to other aspects of the technique, see Paskevska, *Both Sides of the Mirror* (1981).

Batterie. "Battery." A term for all allegro steps in which the legs strike against each other in the air.

Petite batterie. "Little beats." A general term used to describe the little jumps vocabulary which includes all *entrechats brisés* as well as *jeté battu* and *assemblé battu.*

Grand batterie. "Big beats." Describes big jumps like *cabriole* and *entrechat-six de volé.*

Big Poses. *See Arabesque, Attitude*

Bourrée, pas de. A step in three counts of peasant French origin.

Dessous. (1) The back leg initiates the action of stepping up onto *demi-pointe*, the second leg opens and steps to the side, the first leg closes in front. (2) The front leg opens to the side before being brought into 5th position back and stepped upon, the second leg opens to the side, the first leg closes in front. Both versions can be performed *en tournant (en dehors).*

Dessus. (1) The front leg steps up onto *demi-pointe*, the second leg opens and steps to the side, the first leg closes in the back. (2) The back leg opens to the side before being brought into 5th position front and stepped upon, the second leg opens and steps to the side, the first leg closes in the back. Both versions can be performed *en tournant (en dedans).*

En balançoire. "In a rocking fashion." In this version, the feet do not change; the front foot remains in front and the back in the back. Generally performed in an *effacé* position: open back leg to a low *en l'air* extension; *demi-plié* on the other leg, bring working leg to 5th position in the back while rising on *demi-pointe*; step out onto the front leg into a 4th position; bring the back leg into 5th still on *demi-pointe*, then *demi-plié* onto it while opening the front leg to a low *devant* position. Repeat in reverse by bringing the front leg into 5th, stepping out into 4th with the back leg, bring the front leg into 5th on *demi-pointe*, and open the back leg into the low extension while doing a *demi-plié* on the front leg. The arms are the same as for *ballotté*: alternating in 4th *devant*, opposite arm to the front leg when the extension is to the front and same arm as the front leg when the extension is to the back.

Pas de bourrée couru. "Running *bourrée*." This step is generally used as preparatory to a big jump like a *grand jeté*. Three quick steps forward, the first two stepping through a *demi-pointe* the last into a *demi-plié* on the front leg.

Brisé. "Broken, splintered." A low, beaten, traveled *assemblé.*

En avant. From 5th position, the other leg opens to a low *en l'air* position to the side in an *écarté* direction. The back leg from a *demi-plié* pushes off the floor, beats back then front as the landing occurs; the body leans forward over the extended leg, the arms are in 4th *devant* in opposition to the front leg. The step is repeated in the same direction. The step travels forward.

En arrière. From 5th position the front leg opens in an *effacé derrière* position. After the push off the second leg beats front then back as the landing occurs. The arms are in 4th complementary position (same arm in front as front leg), the back is strongly arched and the head turned toward the front. The step is repeated in the same direction. The step travels back.

Brisé volé. "Flying *brisé*." This step can be performed close to the floor, but is most spectacular when executed with a high jump, the beat occurring as the legs are lifted at an angle close to 90 degrees, the body arching forward and back.

From a *dégagé derrière* preparation (in *croisé*),

the back leg describes a *rond de jambe en dedans* as the supporting leg pushes off the floor. The legs meet in the air, the original back leg beats front then back, the landing occurring on that leg, the second leg extended in a low *devant en l'air* position. The arms are in *allongé* position, the opposite arm to the front leg extended forward, the other to the side, the body leans forward over the leg.

The front leg now describes a *rond de jambe en dehors*, the legs meet in the air in the back. The original front leg beats back then front and the other leg extends in a low *derrière* position at the moment of landing. The arms are extended in a high *allongé* in 2nd position and the back arches strongly backward. The movement is repeated. Like the *brisé en avant* it travels forward on a diagonal line. This version can also be done without the *rond de jambe*, the leg opening to the side instead, and the landing occurring with the working leg in a *demi-jambe* position.

Cabriole. "Caper," like a goat's jump. This jump is generally preceded by a *glissade* or a *failli* as preparation. The working leg is lifted in a strong *battement*, the second leg joins it the air with a beat, propelling it higher as the landing occurs.

Cabriole fermée. After the landing has occurred the working leg quickly returns to 5th position.

Cabriole ouverte. After the landing the working leg remains in an extension and the next step is usually a *temps levé-tombé*.

Cabriole derrière. The back leg is lifted in the back, the supporting leg pushes off, beats the uplifted leg in front and the landing occurs on the front leg, the other extended *derrière*.

Cabriole devant. From a *failli* preparation, the back leg swings forward, the other leg pushes off and beats the uplifted leg in the back, and propels it higher as the landing occurs. The arms are in 4th position (oppositional).

Cabriole de côté. Executed in a low *en l'air* position to the side. From 5th position the back leg opens to the side, the other leg pushes off the floor and beats the uplifted leg in the back, the working leg closes in front after the landing has occurred. Generally only executed in a *dessus* manner.

Cambré. "Arched." A bending of the body. *Cambré* is performed forward, back, side, as well as *en rond* (passing through forward, side and back positions smoothly).

Cambré en avant. In 5th position, arms in 2nd, bend the body over until the head is at the height of the knees. The arms move to 5th. Return to vertical keeping the arms in 5th.

Cambré en arrière. In 5th position, arms in 5th, bend the body back, beginning with the head and upper spine, keeping the neck supported. After the full extent of the back bend is reached return to vertical, the arms opening to 2nd as the body reaches full upright. The head follows the front arm, turning toward it as the arm opens to 2nd.

Cambré de côté. In 5th position, one arm up in 5th, the other in *bras bas*. Bend sideways, away from the uplifted arm, the head is turned to look toward the floor.

Note: All the *cambrés* can be performed in other positions besides the 5th: in *dégagé* to *pointe tendue* in all directions, as well as with extensions *en l'air*.

Révérence cambrée. With an extension to *pointe tendue croisé devant*, supporting leg on *demi-plié*, the arms in 4th (oppositional). The body bends forward and spirals, the back shoulder coming forward, the other side of the body moving back. The front arm extends into *allongé*, the other continues the line of the shoulder. The head looks over the front arm. The angle of the arms duplicates the line of the extended leg, like parallel railroad tracks.

Changement battu. *See Royale*

Changement de pieds. "Changing feet." From 5th position, spring up and change the position of the feet from front to back. The landing is on both feet, the original front foot is now in the back.

Chaînés. "Linked like a chain." A series of turns in the same direction, with feet placed in 1st position on *demi-* or full *pointe*. The weight shifts from one foot to the other with each half-revolution. Arms are generally held in 1st position.

Chassé. "Chasing." One foot "chases" the other; it can be done *en avant*, *en arrière*, or *de côté*.

Chassé en avant. With a small jump, the back leg comes to join the front leg in the air, the landing occurs on the back leg but the weight is quickly transferred to the front leg in wide 4th position. The movement is repeated. Arms are in 4th position oppositional.

Chassé en arrière. The front leg, with a small jump, joins the back leg in the air. The landing occurs on the front leg, and transfers to the back leg in order to repeat the movement. The arms are in 4th position (oppositional).

Chassé de côté. The front leg opens to the side, the back leg joins it in the air (with a small jump). The landing occurs on the back leg and transfers to the front leg in order to repeat the movement. The arms are held in 2nd and the movement travels to the side.

Note: The legs do not change, the front remaining in front, and the back leg joining it in the back.

Chassé à terre. Usually used in adagio combinations. From 5th position, one leg slides out to an open position, either 4th or 2nd, both legs are in *demi-plié*. The weight transfers onto the opening leg, the other one extended in *pointe tendue*. The movement can be performed *en avant, en arrière,* and *de côté.*

Chat, pas de. "Step of the cat." From 5th position the back leg is raised to a *retiré* position, the other leg pushes off and also rises to a *retiré* position, at that moment both feet are off the floor. The landing occurs on the first leg, the second leg closes in front as soon as the landing has occurred. The movement can be repeated in the same direction, the feet do not change. The arms are held in 4th *devant*, the body leaning slightly forward and toward the direction of travel.

Russian pas de chat. Same movement as above but the first leg opens to the side and remains straight. Some versions combine the two manners of executions, the first leg opening out straight but bending in a quick *raccourci* movement before landing or, conversely, it begins with a *retiré* position and straightens out to the extension before the landing occurs. The action of the second leg is the same in all versions.

Cheval, pas de. "Step of the horse." A small pawing movement of the leg, punctuated by a small hop on the supporting leg. The step is also performed on *pointe*. The working leg executes a *petit développé* to a *pointe tendue devant,* then the leg bends and lifts in the pawing motion followed closely by a little hop, then another pawing. Weight is then transferred onto the working leg with a little hop and the movement is repeated on the other leg.

Ciseaux, pas de. "Scissors step." A jump in which both legs are thrust in a *grand battement devant.* Usually preceded by a *failli*, from the 4th position the back leg is lifted to the front, the other leg pushes off the floor and in turn executes a *grand battment devant,* passing the first leg in the air. The landing is onto the first leg, the other held up in the air. The body leans slightly back. The arms rise through 1st position to 5th and open out at the moment of landing.

Cloche, en. "As a bell;" a rocking motion. Qualifies *grand battement* when the body tilts forward and back as the leg extends back and front, passing through 1st position. The body leans away from the extended leg, forward when the leg is *derrière,* and arches back when the leg extends to the front.

Contretemps, demi-. "Against time." A composite step which is syncopated, hence its name. From 5th position the back leg opens slightly to the back and bypassing the supporting leg comes to the front. The two legs meet in the air then the second leg (in the back now) passes through a small *retiré* to extend forward into *tombé* (first leg lands first).

Côté, de. See Directions

Cou-de-pied, sur le. A position of the working foot on the supporting ankle. The working foot is flexed and wrapped around the ankle when the heel is in front (*devant* position), and is winged, only the heel touching the supporting ankle, when the position is *derrière.*

Coupé. "To cut." A movement used to free the supporting leg for action, shifting the weight onto the working leg. From a *demi-jambe* position the working foot is brought down so that the other leg can executive the next motion, like an *assemblé*, in which case, the free leg opens into an extension and executes the *assemblé.*

Coupé dessous. *Coupé* under. The working leg in *demi-jambe* position in the back is brought down in the back, freeing the front leg.

Coupé dessus. *Coupé* over. The front leg is in *demi-jambe* position and is brought down in front, freeing the back leg.

Croisé. See Epaulement

Croix, en. "In the shape of a cross." Describes a series of movements that are repeated with the same leg to the front, side, back, and side. The term is used only when the same sequence is repeated in each direction.

Cuisses, temps de. "Step of the thighs." A composite step including a little *passé* through a low *retiré* position, supporting leg on *demi-plié*, and small *sissonne de côté* without changing feet.

Dessous. The front leg passes through *retiré* and comes down in 5th back in *demi-plié*. Immediately both legs push off the floor in a very small *sissonne de côté*, the back leg closes in 5th back.

Dessus. Same action as above but the back leg initiates the motion passing to the front and *sissonne* is executed with the front leg.

Dedans, en. *See* Directions

Dégagé. "To disengage." The working leg opens either to a *pointe tendue* position or to an *en l'air* position. The term is usually used to describe a preparatory movement. The motion can be performed in all directions.

Dehors, en. *See* Directions

Demi-jambe. A position halfway between the knee and the ankle when the working leg is lifted in a *retiré*.

Demi-pointe. *See Pointe*

Derrière. A position of the leg to the back either *par terre* or *en l'air*.

Descendant, en. *See* Directions

Dessous. "Under." A movement performed from 5th front to 5th back.

Dessus. "Over." A movement performed from 5th back to 5th front.

Détourné. "To turn away." From a *relevé* onto both feet in 5th position, a full or half turn is executed, turning toward the back leg. As the swivel occurs, the back leg comes to the front. Can also be used to describe a *promenade* when the position changes from an extension to a *retiré*. For example: from an *arabesque*, as the slow turn begins the leg is brought to *retiré* and as the turn concludes the leg opens into another extension.

Devant. A position of the leg in front, either *par terre* or *en l'air*.

Développé. "To unfold." The working leg is raised to a *retiré* position, then straightens to a full extension to 90 degrees or higher. The movement can be done in all directions.

Diagonal, en. *See* Directions

Directions:
  En avant. "Traveling forward." Qualifies a movement executed in a foward path.
  En arrière. "Traveling backward." Qualifies a movement executed in a backward path.
  De côté. "To the side." Describes either a movement to the side or a motion taking the dancer sideways across the stage.

  En dedans. "Inward." A movement which brings the leg from the back to the front, as in *rond de jambe par terre*. Also any turn which revolves away from the working leg, either *pirouette* or *promenade*.
  En dehors. "Outward." A movement which brings the leg from the front to the back. Also any turn which revolves toward the working leg.
  En montant. "Ascending." Describes a series of steps which bring the dancer closer to upstage. Can be used interchangeably with the term *dessous*.
  En descendant. "Descending." Describes a series of steps which bring the dancer closer to downstage. Can be used interchangeably with the term *dessus*.
  Note: Both the terms, *en descendant* and *en montant* refer to the time when all stages were raked, slanting downward toward the audience. Therefore when the dancer moved downstage he was also "descending."
  Par terre. "On the floor." Describes a position or movement when the pointed toes of the working leg maintain contact with the floor, as in *pointe tendue*, or *rond de jambe par terre*.
  En l'air. "In the air;" lifted off the floor. The term generally refers to a straight leg lifted up to 45 or 90 degrees, like *rond de jambe en l'air* or *devant en l'air*.
  En tournant. "Turning" or involving a spin. Qualifies any movement to which a revolution is added, like *pas de bourrée en tournant*, or *temps levé en tournant*.
  En diagonal. On a diagonal line from one corner to the opposite corner.
  En manège. "In a circle." A series of steps which cover the stage in a circular path. The *manège* usually starts in the left downstage corner for movements to the right, goes across the stage, upstage, across to the third corner, then either downstage and across once more to finish in the right downstage corner, or from the third corner cuts a diagonal which ends in the downstage right corner. For movements to the left, the *manège* starts in the downstage corner right and moves anti-clockwise. Traditionally, the vocabulary used for *manège* includes, for women: *piqués en tournant* both *en dehors* and *en dedans*, *chaînés*, *emboîtés en tournant*, and *grands jetés*; for men: *sauts de basque en tournant*, *grands jetés*, and *grands jetés en tournant*. However, any sequence which repeats to the same side can be used *en manège*.

Ecarté. *See Epaulement*

Echappé. "To escape." A jump from a closed

position (1st or 5th) into an open position (2nd or 4th), and a jump back into the closed position.

Effacé. *See Epaulement*

Elancé. "Darting." Qualifies steps like *grand jeté* when a quick, lengthened movement is required.

Emboîté. "Fitted in," like putting into a box. A jump from one foot to the other, the working leg lifted in a low *attitude* position either in front or behind.

Emboîté en tournant. The body revolves half a turn with each jump, the leg coming to a *demi-jambe* position in front of the supporting leg during each jump. The arms alternate in 4th position *devant* (complementary, i.e., the same arm as the working leg comes to the front).

Enchaînement. "Linked like a chain." Describes a series of steps linked into a dance phrase. Generally refers to *allegro* sequences.

Entrechat. "Cross-caper." A jump which involves a crossing and bypassing of the legs from front to back. The landing can occur on two legs as well as on one with the other leg in a *demi-jambe* position.

Entrechat-trois. This *entrechat* lands on one leg. After the push-off the floor the legs beat once without changing then the working leg assumes the *demi-jambe* position. *Entrechat dessous:* from 5th position, the front leg beats front then passes to *demi-jambe derrière* for the landing. *Entrechat dessus:* from 5th position the back leg beats back then passes to the front to finish in *demi-jambe devant.*

Entrechat-quatre. This *entrechat* lands on both feet. From 5th position the front leg beats back then to the closed position front before landing.

Entrechat-cinq. Like *entrechat-trois*, this movement finishes on one leg, the working leg in *demi-jambe* position. *Entrechat-cinq dessus:* From 5th position the front leg passes to beat in the back then returns to beat in front before landing in *demi-jambe* position front. *Entrechat-cinq dessous:* From 5th position the back leg passes to beat in front, then back before landing in *demi-jambe* position in the back.

Entrechat-cinq volé. This movement is a beaten *assemblé*. The working leg after opening in a high *seconde* beats front, back, and returns to front for the landing. The *assemblé* is preceded by a *failli* or a *glissade* and travels on a diagonal, the arms in an *allongé* position, the body in *écarté.*

Entrechat-six. Like *entrechat-quatre*, entre-chat-six finishes on both feet. From 5th position the front leg passes to beat back then front, and back again before landing.

Note: In all *entrechats*, both the passing and the beating are counted, which gives the numbering, i.e., *entrechat-quatre*: 1—passing by opening the legs slightly sideways; 2—beat back; 3—passing; 4—beat front.

Epaulé. *See Epaulement*

Epaulement. "Shouldered." Subtle shifts of the torso which accompany positions of the legs. Arms and head positions are included in each pose.

Croisé. "Crossed over." A position qualifying front or back directions of the leg which in its extension crosses over the central line of the body. The arms are usually in 4th oppositional, the head is tilted and turned toward the front arm.

Ecarté. "Stretched out widely apart." A position qualifying directions of the leg to the side. In *écarté devant* the direction of the leg is slightly in front of the true *seconde*, the body aligned to the same diagonal. The arms are in 4th complementary. The head is turned and tilted up toward the uplifted arm.

In *écarté derrière* the direction of the leg is slightly behind the true *seconde*, the body aligned to the same diagonal. The arms are in 4th oppositional. The head is turned toward the front arm, the gaze is downward.

Effacé. "Erased, or shaded." A position qualifying front or back directions of the leg. This movement is away, opened out from the central line of the body. The arms are in 4th oppositional. The head is tilted and turned toward the front arm.

Epaulé. "Shouldered." This term further qualifies a *croisé* position, either front or back. The same arm as the front leg is lifted to 5th, the head is turned and tilted toward the front arm.

En face. "Facing straight forward." In this postion, the arms are held in 2nd, the head and body facing straight front. The working leg can open in all three directions, front, side, or back.

Failli. "Almost" (finish). A composite jump which includes a *sissonne* and a *tombé*.

Note: The French School calls this step *sissonne-tombé*.

En avant. From 5th position, push off both legs as for a *sissonne*, in the air the back leg opens into a low *arabesque*. The landing occurs on the front leg and the back leg swings forward through 1st position into a *tombé en avant* in a wide 4th position, the front leg in *demi-plié*, the back leg extended. This step is used as preparation for a variety of jumps.

En arrière. From 5th position, after the initial push off, the front leg opens to a low *devant* position then swings to the back. The back leg is in *demi-plié*, the front leg extended. Probably due to its awkwardness this step is seldom used.

Fermé. "Closed." Qualifies some jumps which usually finish in an open position, such as *jeté fermé*, indicating that the movement ends by closing the working leg into 5th position.

Flèche, temps de. "Step of the arrow." Usually preceded by a *failli*, the back leg swings through 1st position to a *grand battement devant*, at the same time the other leg pushes off the floor and does *développé devant*, passing the first leg in the air, like an arrow being shot through a bow. The arms rise through the movement to 5th position and open out at the moment of landing when the body leans slightly back, the second leg still extended in a high *devant* position.

Flic-flac. A step introduced into the vocabulary by the Russian School. From a low extension in *seconde*, the working foot brushes against the floor in front then back of the working leg while the body revolves (*en dedans*); the working leg then opens to the extended position in *seconde*. The step is reversed by brushing back then front as the body revolves (*en dehors*). The brush is executed by the metatarsals, the toes flexed, the heel lifted off the floor. The supporting leg rises to a low *demi-pointe* position, just high enough for the spin to occur. The movement ends on a full *demi-pointe*.

Fondu. *See Battement fondu*

Fouetté. "To whip." Generally refers to a movement which is executed by turning the body either toward or away from an extended working leg. Additionally the term is used to describe some *pirouettes* when the working leg whips into a *retiré* position.

Fouetté en dedans. The working leg is extended in a high *devant* position, the supporting leg is in *demi-plié*. With a *relevé* the body turns away from the leg, the movement finishing in *arabesque*. The movement can also be performed with a revolution of the body, either half a turn or full turn, and can be executed in *croisé* or *effacé* directions (*fouetté en tournant*).

Fouetté en dedans (pirouettes). From a wide 4th position, front leg on *demi-plié* back leg straight, arms in 4th *devant* (complementary). The back leg pushes off and opens to *seconde*,

then with a *relevé* on the supporting leg, the working leg whips into a *retiré* position. The arms open into 2nd as the leg travels to *seconde*, then rise to 5th. The spin finishes with the working leg closing front either in 4th or in 5th. *Fouetté en dedans* is also used in a series linked by *fouettés en dehors*: After the initial preparation, a *fouetté en dehors* is executed, the spin ends with a *coupé dessus*, freeing the back leg to open to the side and execute a *fouetté en dedans* ending with a *coupé dessous*, which frees the front leg to open to the side for the next *fouetté en dehors*. These series can also be performed with three *fouettés en dehors* and one *fouetté en dedans*.

Fouetté en dedans en tournant. Often preceded by a *failli*, the working leg swings forward in a *grand battement* to 90 degrees, the arms rise to 5th, and the supporting leg does a *relevé* to *demi-* or full *pointe*. The body turns sharply away from the working leg into first *arabesque*. Another *relevé* follows in the *arabesque*, the arms opening to 2nd position. Then the working leg swings to *devant*, the arms rising to 5th, and the body turns away from the leg while a half turn or a full turn is executed, the movement finishes again in first *arabesque* and can be repeated, omitting the *failli-fouetté*.

Note: The working leg is carried in front until the final direction has been almost reached, then the body executes the *fouetté*, which consists of turning away from the extended leg. In other words, to do a full turn, the leg is carried in front until the body faces the third corner (the first corner is the starting point), then the *fouetté* is executed which brings the body to the starting point again.

Fouetté en dehors. The working leg is extended in an *arabeseque*, the supporting leg is in *demi-plié*. With a *relevé* the body turns toward the uplifted leg ending the movement with the leg extended in front. Like the *fouetté en dedans*, this one can be performed *en tournant*.

Fouetté en dehors (pirouettes). Usually preceded by a *pirouette en dehors* as a preparation, then the working leg opens to the front, the supporting leg on *demi-plié*, and whips to the side and into *retiré* as the supporting leg rises on *pointe*. The *pirouette* occurs as the leg whips into *retiré*. A series is generally executed, from sixteen to thirty-two turns, although a few dancers have been known to exceed the legendary thirty-two *fouettés*.

Grand fouetté. "Big whipping." The *fouetté* movements are the exact opposite of *rond de jambe* movements; in *rond de jambe* the leg circles the body; in *fouettés* the body turns away or toward the leg. *En dehors*: with the leg in an extension to the back at 90 degrees, the body rotates toward the stationary leg until the leg is in an extension to the front and the body faces the other side. *En dedans*: with the leg in an extension to the front, the body rotates away from the leg ending in a *derrière* position facing the other way.

Frappés.   *See Battement frappé*

Gargouillade.   "Gurgling or rumbling." This jump is generally preceded by a *coupé dessous* and consists of a *pas de chat* with *ronds de jambe en l'air* during the jump. Following the *coupé*, the front leg opens to a low *seconde* and executes a *double rond en dehors*; the back leg pushes off as the front leg opens and executes a *double rond en dedans*. The two legs slightly overlap. The second leg closes in front.

Glissade.   "Slide or glide." A linking or preparatory step in which one leg opens to a *pointe tendue*, the other leg on *demi-plié*, then weight is transferred to first leg, the other pointing to *pointe tendue*, the movement ends by the second leg sliding into 5th position.
   En avant.   The front leg opens to the front, the other leg on *demi-plié*, weight transfers onto the front leg which does a *demi-plié*, the back leg extending to *pointe tendue*. The back leg closes in 5th in the back.
   En arrière.   The back leg opens to the back and the movement above is reversed.
   De côté sans changé.   Either the front or the back leg opens to the side and the closing returns the legs to their original positions.
   De côté changé.   In this movement the legs change position at the end, the front leg finishing back and vice versa.
   Précipité.   "Hurried." This *glissade* is executed quickly without a wide extension, and is used as preparation for jumps or *piqués* onto *pointe*.

Glissé.   "To glide or slide."

Jeté.   "Thrown." A jump which begins on one leg and land on the other.
   Jeté dessous.   From 5th position, the front leg opens to a low *seconde*, the second leg pushes off and assumes a *demi-jambe* position in front as the landing occurs on the first leg.
   Jeté dessus.   In contrast to the *grand jeté*, this *jeté* is small and is part of the *petit allegro* vocabulary. From 5th position the back leg opens to a low *seconde*, the second leg pushes off and assumes a *demi-jambe* position in the back, as the landing occurs on the first leg.

Grand jeté.   Usually preceded by a *glissade* or a *pas de bourrée couru*, the most common form of this *jeté* is *en avant*: the front leg does a *grand battement devant* at the same time as the back leg pushes off the floor propelling the body upward. In the air the legs are in a split position, one leg in front, one in the back. The landing is onto the front leg. This *jeté* can also be executed into an *attitude* position, the front leg is straight and the back one is lifted into *attitude*, landing in *attitude*.
   The *grand jeté* can also be done *de côté*, the legs kicking up into a wide *seconde* in the air; this version is generally a *jeté fermé*: the second leg closes in 5th after the landing has occurred. The last version is *en arrière*: the back leg does a *grand battement* and the front leg pushes off and extends to the front, the landing is onto the back leg. This *jeté* is seldom performed.
   Grand jeté en tournant.   Usually preceded by a *pas de bourrée couru* upstage from a downstage corner (on a diagonal). The first leg does a *grand battement devant*, the second leg pushes off at the same time as the body revolves in the air, the legs pass each other in the air, the first leg on its way down and the second leg on its way to *arabesque*. The landing is onto the first leg, the other in *arabesque*. This *jeté* can also include a beat as the legs pass each other in the air and is then called *entrelacé*: "interlaced."

Levé, temps.   "Lifting step." A hop which occurs after a position has been assumed. It can be performed in any position, but most frequently follows a *jeté dessus* or *dessous*, it can also be used after a *chassé* as in *chassé temps levé* in *arabesque*.

Lié, temps.   "Linked step." Describes the linking motion between two positions, a *demi-plié* through 2nd or 4th which transfers the weight of the body from one leg to the other. Also describes an exercise which is used to promote weight transference and coordination between arms and legs. The exercise can be done to a *pointe tendue* (see Year Six) as well as to *en l'air* positions (*arabesque*, *seconde*, *devant en l'air*).

Manège, en.   *See* Directions

Montant, en.   *See* Directions

Ouvert.   "Open." Qualifies steps and positions when a step ends in an open position, like *sissonne ouverte*; or a position is open in relationship to the audience.

Papillon, pas de.   "Step of the butterfly." Usually

preceded by a *tombé* into a wide 4th position, weight on the front leg. The back leg is lifted in the back as the supporting leg pushes off and also is lifted in the back, both knees are slightly bent. The legs pass each other in the air, the body arches back and the arms dip then lift with the jump into 2nd *allongé* position. The movement ends with the second leg sliding through to the wide 4th *tombé* which began the movement.

Passé. "Passing." Most often associated with *retiré*, when the working leg is lifted to the height of the supporting knee and passes from front to close in the back, or vice versa. Can also describe passing through the *retiré* position from an extension into another.

Passer la jambe. A *grand battement* either to the front or the back, then a passage through a *retiré* to an extension in the opposite direction, i.e., from the front to the back, or from the back to the front.

Penché. "Leaning." *Penché* describes a pose in which the body leans either forward or backward and the working foot is raised high so that the foot is at the highest point.

Piqué. "Pricked," as with a sharp needle. *Piqué* is used to describe a lifting and bouncing off the floor with a fully extended leg, such as *battement jeté piqué*, or *grand battement piqué*, whereby the leg instead of closing in 5th, comes to a *pointe tendue* and is raised again.

Pirouette piquée en dedans. The body is propelled by a push from the back leg onto *pointe* on the front leg. The back leg assumes a *retiré* position in the back of the supporting knee and a *pirouette* is executed. The spin finishes by coming down on the back leg in *demi-plié* and the *piqué* is repeated.

Pirouette piquée en dehors. From a *tombé* into a 4th position to *effacé devant*, the back leg circles around to the front and the back leg pushes off and comes to a *retiré* position while the front leg lands onto *pointe* and a *pirouette* is executed.

Pirouette. "A turn." A spin on *demi-* or full *pointe* of one leg while the other is raised to a specific position, in *retiré* or one of the big poses.

En dedans. A spin away from the working leg. The preparation can be in 5th, 2nd, or 4th positions, although the 4th is most commonly used. The arms are in 4th *devant*, the same arm as the direction of the spin is in front. The arm opens slightly at the moment preceding the *relevé*, then the two arms join in 1st position or

raise up to 5th. The back leg comes into a *retiré* position in front of the supporting knee for the spin and closes in front at the end either in 5th or in 4th.

Note: The working leg, instead of coming directly to the *retiré* can open to *seconde*, the supporting leg on *demi-plié*, then assumes the *retiré* position at the moment of the *relevé* on the supporting leg. This *pirouette* is usually called *fouetté en dedans*.

En dehors. A spin toward the working leg. The preparation for this turn can be in 5th, 2nd, or 4th position. The arms in 4th *devant* (the same arm as the direction of the spin is in front: right arm for right turn, left arm for left turn). The arm opens slightly at the moment preceding the *relevé*, then the two arms join in 1st position for the spin. The working leg comes to a *retiré* position in front of the knee during the spin and finishes in the back either in 4th or 5th position.

Grandes pirouettes. Pirouette in any of the big poses of the vocabulary, either *en dehors* or *en dedans*. The preparation is generally in a wide 4th position. *Pirouette* in *seconde* can start from a 2nd position preparation. The pose is assumed at the moment of the *relevé*.

Plié. "Bending" of the knees. Performed in 1st, 2nd, 3rd, 4th, and 5th positions. *Demi-plié*: halfway to a full bending of the knees, the heels remain on the floor in all positions. *Grand plié*: full bending of the knees. In 2nd and 4th *ouverte* positions the heels remain on the floor; in the other positions the heels are allowed to rise after the depth of the *demi-plié* has been reached. *Plié* is also used as a general term to describe a bending of the supporting knee or knees.

Pointe. "On the toes." The weight rests on the tips of the toes of fully pointed feet.

Demi-pointe. "On half toes," a rise or a position with the toes flexed, the weight resting on the metatarsals, or the ball of the foot.

Pointe tendue. "Pointed stretch." An extended leg in any direction with the toes touching the floor. The term can indicate a position assumed as a preparation or a position assumed after a leg has been lifted in the air.

Poisson, temps de. "Step of the fish." This jump utilizes the action for *failli* and adds a highly arched back at the apex of the jump. The legs are held closely together, the body in a *effacé* direction, the arms in 5th position, the head turned toward the front. At the moment of landing, the back leg lifts into *arabesque* then swings forward onto a *tombé croisé*.

Polka. A step in three counts. The first count is a hop on one leg as the other leg executes a *petit développé*. Weight is transferred onto the working leg and is followed by a *chassé*. Then the other leg comes through with a little hop. Can be performed *en avant*, *en arrière*, and *de côté*.

Port de bras. "Movement of the arms" from one position to the other.
First port de bras. From *bras bas*, through lst position and opening to 2nd.
Second port de bras. From *bras bas* through lst position to 5th, the arms return to *bras bas* through 2nd.
Third port de bras. From *bras bas* through lst position to 3rd, the front arm opening to 2nd to assume 4th position, then through 2nd position to *bras bas*.
Grand port de bras. In deep 4th position arms in 4th oppositional. The body bends forward over the supporting leg then circles to the side toward the uplifted arm which opens to 2nd and the other arm rises to 5th. The body continues the rotation by bending to the back, then return to upright as the second arm returns to 2nd position and the first arm returns to 5th (the same position as at the start of the motion). The weight of the body is maintained on the front leg throughout.
Port de bras en rond. From a *pointe tendue* position, *derriére croisé*, arms in 4th oppositional. The body bends forward as the back heel is brought down and both legs are in *demi-plié* in a shallow 4th position. The body continues the rotation by bending to the side, the first arm goes to 2nd, the second arm rises to 5th and the weight is shifted onto the back leg with the front leg in *pointe tendue croisé devant*. The body continues its rotation by going to the back, then returns to upright while the first arm returns to 5th and the second arm opens to 2nd.
Note: In all *port de bras*, the movement of the head follows the movement of the arms: Looking into the hands in 1st position and turning toward the front arm when the arms open to 2nd or rise to 5th. During the *grand port de bras* and *port de bras en rond*, the head's focus is straight out and down when the body bends forward, then it follows the first arm (in 5th); when the second arm is brought to 5th the head follows it, in that manner continuing the rotation and finishes with the focus toward the audience (4th position).

Porté. "Carried." Usually refers to a partnered pose when the female dancer is carried by her partner.

Posé. "Placed." Describes the action of stepping out onto a leg while the other assumes a position, generally *en l'air*, like *posé* into *arabesque*. The *posé* is always onto a flat foot in contrast to a *piqué* which is always onto *demi-* or full *pointe*.

Positions. There are five positions of the feet. A sixth was named by Serge Lifar, the feet in parallel position, which is used in Character Dance. The balletic positions are: 1st, heels together; 2nd, feet apart by the distance of a foot-and-a-half; 3rd, one heel in front of the other; 4th, one foot directly in front of the other by the distance of a foot; 5th, the feet are placed toe-to-heel, the front foot fitting snuggly against the back foot.
Note: The 4th position can be executed either in the crossed over version — opposite 5th position, or in the *ouverte* position — opposite 1st position. When *grands pliés* are performed in 4th *ouverte*, the heels do not leave the floor, duplicating the action of a plié in 2nd position.

Promenade. A movement on one leg, the other raised, whereby the body rotates around the central point of the foot on the floor. The position assumed for the *promenade* is maintained, the rotation effected by the movement of the supporting heel shifting forward in *promenade en dedans*, and shifting back in *promenade en dehors*. Also refers to partnered vocabulary when the man walks around, rotating his partner who balances on one *pointe*, the other leg lifted in a big pose. The man holds his partner either by the waist or by the hands or by one hand as in *promenade* in *attitude*.

Raccourci. *See Battement*

Relevé. "Lifted." Describes a movement of a straight leg when lifted off the floor, as in *battement relevé*. Also refers to the springing motion onto *demi-* or full *pointe* either on one leg or on both, as in *relevé passé* (on one foot) or *sous-sus* (on both feet).

Renversé. "Turned upside down." A composite step which involves a turn.
En dedans. From an extension to *seconde* or a first *arabesque croisée*, the working leg comes to a high *retiré* position while the supporting leg sinks into a *demi-plié*, the body bends toward the lifted leg sideway, and the arms are in 1st position. A swivel is executed in this position finishing with a high extension into *seconde*, the body leaning away from the extended leg, the arms in 2nd, the sequence ends with a *pas de bourrée dessous*.
En dehors. From a *tombé en avant croisé*,

coupé with the back leg, then the front leg executes a *grand rond de jambe* as the supporting leg does a *relevé* to *demi-pointe*. The *rond de jambe* finishes either in *arabesque* or in *attitude croisée*, the back highly arched. The arms, for finishing in *arabesque*, rise to 5th and open to 2nd when the *arabesque* is reached; for finishing in *attitude* the arms open to 2nd then the same arm as the working leg rises to 5th (4th position oppositional). The *rond* can finish either on *demi-pointe* or in *demi-plie*, then a quick *pas de bourrée en tournant* follows with both versions.

Retiré. "Taken away." Describes the movement of one leg as it is lifted with a bent knee, until the toes are level with the supporting knee or level with the calf for *demi-jambe* position. The toes generally touch the supporting knee in front, as in all *pirouettes* except *piqué en dedans* when the foot is placed in the back of the calf.

Revoltade. "A turn about." This is a composite jump, a *grand jeté en tournant* ending with a *fouetté en dehors*. After the apex of the jump has been reached, the body turns toward the leg extended in *derrière* position, and the jump lands on one leg the other extended *en l'air devant*; it can finish either in *effacé* or *croisé* the arms in 4th oppositional.

Rond de Jambe. "Circle of the leg." *Rond de jambe* is used in combination with other movements.

Rond de jambe par terre. Circling of the working leg, the toes never leaving the floor. *En dehors:* the motion starts in front, passes through second position to end in the back. It passes through first position to extend again in front, and the movement is repeated. *En dedans:* the motion starts in the back, proceeds through second position to the front, then through first position to the back to continue the circlings. Can also be executed with a *demi-plié* on the supporting leg.

Rond de jambe en l'air. "Circle of the leg in the air." The working leg opens to 90 degrees to the side; with the thigh held in place the lower leg bends toward the supporting knee to describe a small circle, then extends again to 90 degrees before closing in 5th position. *En dedans:* from 5th position back, the leg opens and describes the circle, moving slightly forward, then back, and open again to a full extension before lowering to 5th position front. *En dehors:* from 5th position front, the leg extends to 90 degrees, the circling brings the lower leg slightly back then forward; the knee straightens to a full extension, and the leg closes back.

Note: *Rond de jambe en l'air* can also be performed at 45 degrees at a faster speed — one count for each rond.

Grand rond de jambe en l'air. "Big circling with the leg in the air." *En dehors: développé* to the front, then the leg is carried smoothly through *seconde* to *derrière* position, the height is maintained through the entire motion. *En dedans: développé* to the back, then the leg is carried through *seconde* to *devant* position.

Royale. "Royal." This term is used to describe the striking together of the calves. Also called a *changement battu*.

Sauté. "Jumped." Qualifies movements that can be done with a jump, like *rond de jambe sauté* or *foutté sauté*.

Seconde. A position of the leg to the side, either *par terre* or *en l'air*.

Sissonne. Unlike the majority of the terms, this step derives its name from the dancer who is reputed to have created it, *Comte de Sissone*. A jump from both feet onto one, the second leg opening to an *en l'air* position then closing in 5th after the landing has occurred.

Sissonne en avant. From 5th position after the take off the back leg opens into *arabesque* then closes in 5th; the step travels a little forward.

Sissonne en arrière. From 5th position after the take off the front leg opens to *devant en l'air* then closes in 5th front; the step travels a little back.

Sissonne de côté. Dessus: From 5th position, the back leg opens after the take off to a low *seconde* position then closes in front. *Dessous:* From 5th position the front leg opens after the take off to a low *seconde* position then closes in the back. The step travels a little to the side, away from the opening leg.

Sissonne ordinaire. Ordinary *sissonne* (a Cecchetti term): A jump from both feet with the working leg coming to *demi-jambe* position either in front or behind the supporting leg as the landing occurs.

Sissonne ouverte. Into *arabesque*: After the initial takeoff, the back leg passes through a *retiré* position and does a *développé* into *arabesque*. This step is usually done on a diagonal finishing in an open *arabesque*, arms in 4th position oppositional. Into *seconde*: From 5th position the front leg executes the *développé*, arms in 4th (same arm lifted as leg *en l'air*), the body leaning away from the extended leg, the head turned away from the extended leg. This version is usually followed by a *coupé dessous*, *assemblé dessous*, and travels on a straight line across the room.

176

Soubresaut. "Sudden jump." From 5th position, this jump is executed from both feet onto both feet without changing, the same leg staying in front. It can travel forward, side, or back as well as be executed on place. The legs are held close together during the jump.

Sous-sus. "Under-over." Describes the position of the legs in 5th and is a *relevé* onto both feet either on *demi-* or *full pointe*.

Soutenu. "Sustained." From 5th position one leg opens to *pointe tendue*, supporting leg on *demi-plié*, the first leg comes back into 5th as a *relevé* on both legs occurs.

    Soutenu en tournant en dehors. The front leg opens to *pointe tendue* in 2nd then is brought to 5th behind the supporting leg, both legs rise to *demi-pointe*, a swivel begins toward the back leg whereby the back foot shifts to front, the turn is completed keeping the front foot in front. Arms open to 2nd with the extension, then pass through *bras bas* and rise to 5th.

    Soutenu en tournant en dedans. The back leg opens to 2nd, supporting leg on *demi-plié*, then the leg is brought to 5th in front, the swivel occurs again toward the back foot with the change of feet during the turn. The arms are the same as above. Both *soutenus* can be done on *pointe* in which case a little spring (*relevé*) occurs when the two legs are brought together.

Temps. ("Step"). *See Flèche, Levé, Lié*

Terre à terre. "Close to the floor." Describes steps that stay close to the floor even if jumped.

Tombé. "Fall." A transference of weight onto one leg which frees the other leg for action. The fall is preceded by the opening of the working leg to an *en l'air* position often accompanied by rise to *demi-pointe* on the supporting leg. It can be done in all directions.

    Tombé en avant. From an extension to the front the weight is dropped onto the front leg which sinks in a *demi-plié*, the other leg extended in the back either *pointe tendue* or with the heel on the floor in a wide 4th position.

    Tombé en arrière. From an extension to the back, the weight is dropped onto the back leg which sinks in a *demi-plié*. The other leg is extended in a *pointe tendue devant*.

    Tombé de côté. From an extension to the side, the weight is dropped onto the working leg which sinks in a *demi-plié*, the other leg is extended in a *pointe tendue à la seconde*.

Tour en l'air. "Turn in the air." From a 5th position the push off occurs from both feet, the *tour* is *en dehors*—toward the front leg which slips to the back during the revolution in the air. The *tour* can finish in 5th or 4th position, it can also end on one knee (back knee), or in one of the big poses, *arabesque*, or *attitude*. It is usually preceded by a preparatory step like *sous-sus* or *assemblé*.

Tour de reins. Reins are kidneys. The movement consists of a *coupé* as preparation and a *grand jeté* which is turned in the air: the first leg does a *grand battement* to the front in an *effacé* direction, the second leg pushes off, in the air the split position of the legs is enhanced by a highly arched back, the landing occurs on the front leg the body now facing *croisé* on the other side. The back leg can be lifted in an *attitude* position or an *arabesque*.

Tournant, en. *See* Directions

Tourné. "Turned, or spun." Qualifies steps both *terre à terre* and *en l'air*, denoting that a spin or revolution is added to the execution of the step.

Volé. See *Assemblé, Brisé, Entrechat-cing*

SELECTED BIBLIOGRAPHY

John Gregory, Nicolas Legat, *Heritage of a Ballet Master.* NY Dance Horizons, 1977

Hammond, Sandra Noll. *Ballet Basics.* Palo Alto, Cal.: Mayfield Publishing Co., 1982.

_____. *Ballet: Beyond the Basics.* Palo Alto, Cal.: Mayfield Publishing Co., 1982.

Karsavina, Tamara. *Ballet Technique.* London: A & C Black, 1956.

_____. *Classical Ballet: The Flow of Movement.* London: A & C Black, 1962.

Kostrovitskaya, Vera, and Alexei Pisarev. *School of Classical Dance.* Translated by John Barker. Moscow: Progress Publishers, 1978.

Lawson, Joan. *Ballet Class: Principles and Practice.* New York: Theatre Arts Books, 1984.

_____. *The Principles of Classical Dance.* New York: Alfred A. Knopf, 1980.

_____. *The Teaching of Classical Ballet.* 2d ed. New York: Theatre Arts Books, 1983.

Manthorp, Beryl. *Towards Ballet: Dance Training for the Very Young.* Princeton: Dance Horizons/Princeton Book Company, 1987.

Mara, Thalia. *First Steps in Ballet: Basic Exercises at the Barre.* Princeton: Dance Horizons/Princeton Book Company, 1987.

_____. *Fourth Steps in Ballet: On Your Toes! Basic Pointe Work.* Princeton: Dance Horizons/Princeton Book Company, 1987.

_____. *The Language of Ballet: A Dictionary.* Princeton: Dance Horizons/Princeton Book Company, 1987.

_____. *Second Steps in Ballet: Basic Center Exercises.* Princeton: Dance Horizons/Princeton Book Company, 1987.

_____. *Third Steps in Ballet: Basic Allegro Steps.* Princeton: Dance Horizons/Princeton Book Company, 1987.

Martyn, Laurel. *Let Them Dance: A Preparation for Dance and Life.* London: Dance Books Ltd., 1985.

Messerer, Asaf. *Classes in Classical Ballet.* Translated by Oleg Briansky. New York: Doubleday & Company, 1975.

Page, Ruth. *Class: Notes on Dance Classes Around the World.* Princeton: Princeton Book Company, 1984.

Paskevska, Anna. *Both Sides of the Mirror: The Science and Art of Ballet.* Princeton: Dance Horizons/Princeton Book Company, 1981.

_____. *Getting Started in Ballet, A Parents Guide to Dance Education.* Oxford University Press, NY 1997.

Serrebrenikov, Nicolai, and Joan Lawson. *The Art of Pas de Deux.* London: Dance Books Ltd., 1978.

Shook, Karel. *Elements of Classical Ballet Technique.* Princeton: Dance Horizons/Princeton Book Company, 1977.

Vaganova, Agrippina. *Basic Principles of Classical Ballet.* Translated by Anatole Chujoy. New York: Dover Books, 1969.

DISCOGRAPHY

Jay Distributors

Lynn Stanford - Ballet Class	80-01
David Howard - Ballet Class	82-01
Another Great Class -	89-14
Music for Ballet Class - Muriel Stuart	84-02

Roper Records

Extended list of music for Ballet class. Especially useful are classes supervised by Mme Halina and David Howard, also one CD with pianist Raymond Wilson who worked at Harkness and later with Maria Tallchief in Chicago.
http://www.roperdancemusic.com
Princeton Book Company Publishers

Music for Ballet Class- Meyer and Paskevska 200016D

Shoeshine Records

Dimitri Roudnev, Marina Stolyar. Music for Ballet Class